Dianne Durand's Complete Book of

SMOCKING

Dianne Durand

PRENTICE HALL PRESS • NEW YORK

ACKNOWLEDGMENTS

I wish to thank Nellie Bass Durand, my dear friend, for the many hours of sharing her ideas, thoughts, and projects. Her teaching experience and designs have given me a wealth of new direction in preparing the text of this book.

Many thanks to Sylvia Coleman for writing an historical synopsis based on her research on smocking.

My appreciation goes to Kathy Kiebzak, Mary Hooks, Alicia Mullins and Mary Leslie Sheeley for letting us photograph their beautiful projects; to Charles Brooks for his innovative photography; and to Betsy and Stuart Worden for opening their home to our crew of models and photography equipment; and

to Irene Small for helping me with the illustrations and the graphs.

This book would never have been finished without the support and help of my loving husband, Roy Gerard, and of Donna Gross, Thein Freeman, and all the ladies who work with me each day at Little Miss Muffet, Inc.

I am most appreciative of the contributions of my editor, Susan Gies, who made it possible to pull this manuscript together.

But most of all I thank Peter and Amanda who have inspired and worn most of the projects in this book. Without them I never would have begun to smock. These are the very special people in my life.

First Prentice Hall Press Edition, 1986
Published by Simon & Schuster, Inc.
Gulf + Western Building
One Gulf + Western Plaza
New York, NY 10023

Originally published by Van Nostrand Reinhold Company Inc.

PRENTICE HALL PRESS is a trademark of Simon & Schuster, Inc.

Library of Congress Cataloging-in-Publication Data
Durand, Dianne.
  Dianne Durand's Complete book of smocking.

  Includes Index.
  1. Smocking. I. Title. II. Title: Complete book of smocking.
TT840.D86   746.44   81-3019
ISBN 0-671-60990-4   AACR2

Manufactured in the United States of America

10 9 8 7 6 5 4 3 2 1

CONTENTS

INTRODUCTION

Smocking is a surface embroidery worked across pleated fabric. It is unique among embroidery forms in that it serves two purposes: first, it provides ornamentation; second, because of its elastic nature, smocking provides a means of controlling a garment's fullness, thereby creating more shape for the wearer.

There are basically two kinds of smocking. The first, that which is referred to as "English smocking," consists of gathering the fabric into close pleats and then, using the gathering threads as a guide, embroidering rows of stitches through the pleats. Once the embroidery has been completed, the gathering threads are pulled out (the pleats are now held in place by the smocking) and the smocking is steamed into shape. With the second kind of smocking, pleating and stitching are done in one step. All you have to do is smock the stitches across the fabric. This method is usually done on gingham. The fabric has less elasticity and the pleats are not as regular. This is also the type of smocking usually found on commercial patterns. The text of this book will deal with English smocking.

The art of smocking evolved from the Anglo-Saxon "smocc." The smocc was a very plain, fairly full, sacklike, knee-length outer garment that was worn over the farmers' other garments to keep them from getting soiled. Although the smocc was considered to be male peasants' occupational garb, women had their own smocked garments too. From the eleventh to the eighteenth centuries, smocking was incorporated into the females' "smicket," which was a loose garment worn next to the skin. (The smicket was called a "chemise" in the eighteenth century.) Since smickets were, therefore, hidden from view, it is no wonder that smocking of that time is associated with the clothing of males.

Lavishly embroidered "peasant smocks" became very popular during the eighteenth and nineteenth centuries, reflecting the improved status of the rural Englishman. The smock was generally made of Holland drill linen and was highly prized, cherished, and often willed to a loved one upon one's death. These smocks were truly amazing costumes. They were made entirely of square- and rectangular-shaped pieces of fabric which were embellished with embroidery over the pleats in the bodice and sleeve areas. The smocking drew the garment in over the body and still allowed it to be very elastic and comfortable for the wearer. The widths of these smocks ranged from five feet to eight yards.

The demise of this beautiful English garment came with the onset of the Industrial Revolution. The introduction of farm machinery posed a safety threat to the farmer in his voluminous smock. The smock began to disappear from the English countrysides. Fortunately, smocking was preserved in the 1870s and 80s by Mrs. Oscar Wilde and her "arty" set who adopted smocking and incorporated it into their dress bodices. Ladies' and children's smocked dresses became specialties of several London and Paris dressmakers. The full styles worn around the turn of the twentieth century lent themselves readily to smocking.

Most people associate smocking with a traditional family heirloom, but smocking is certainly not a thing of the past. Today, we are again experiencing a resurgence of interest in English smocking, although with emphasis on its decorative, rather than functional aspects. Smocking can be used to decorate and personalize garments for every member of the family. The techniques are easy to learn and offer new challenges for both the novice and the more experienced seamstress. Included in this book are all the techniques and skills you will need to become a smocker. Part one will teach you the basic smocking skills. Even if you don't know how to embroider, the diagrams and step-by-step instructions will teach you all the smocking stitches you'll need to make beautiful designs. Part two will tell you how to apply these skills so that you can incorporate smocking in the garments you sew. Part three presents dozens of projects for dresses, shirts, blouses, jackets, and more for men, women, children, and babies.

There are many dimensions of smocking to explore. The more expertise you develop, the more you will want to experiment on your own. Learning the art of smocking enables you to turn your home-made projects into handcrafted heirlooms, while recapturing the charm and enchantment of the past.

This book is the culmination of years of experimenting, designing, and researching smocking techniques. After I began to smock for my baby daughter, I was a "hooked smocker." Today I have many friends and a business that produces smocking supplies.

The goal of this book is to present smocking as a creative art needlework form. As with any art, the first step to creativity is an understanding of the fundamental techniques. I hope this book will illustrate the basic techniques so that anyone can enjoy many hours of productive creativity.

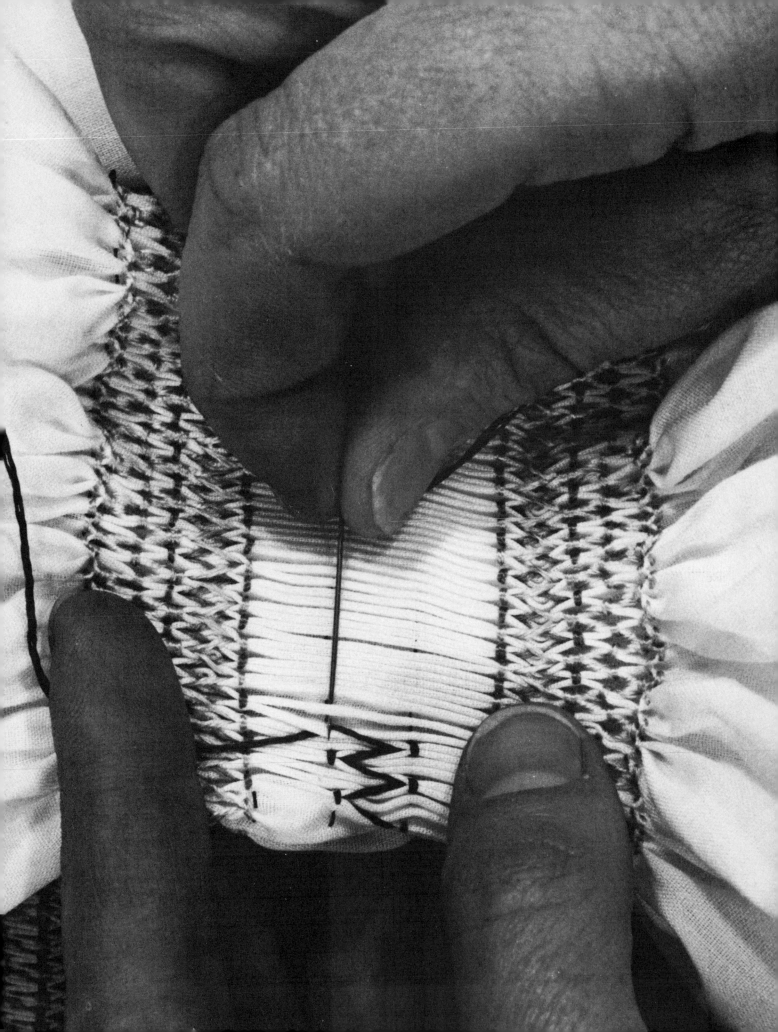

PART ONE

The Basic Techniques of Smocking Art

Smocking is a surface embroidery with both functional and decorative functions. This makes it practical for use in clothing as well as on ornamental accessories. It is elastic, providing shape to the fullness of the fabric. What's more, the extra thickness of the pleats can provide insulation against the cold. The distinctive decorative quality of smocking adds individualized ornamentation to any garment or accessory.

Before you work the smocking stitches, you must gather the fabric into uniform pleats. In addition to holding the pleats, these gathering threads will serve as a guide for the stitching in much the same way that lines on a writing pad are used. There are a number of different embroidery stitches that can be combined to form an endless number of designs.

Once you have completed the design, you will pull out the gathering threads and block the smocked piece into shape. You can then stitch the project together. In a nutshell, there are seven basic steps in smocking:

- choosing material
- cutting out fabric
- gathering pleats
- smocking
- pulling out gathering threads
- blocking
- finishing construction

Choosing Materials

For most projects, you can use a good-quality cotton or cotton blend. Also consider lightweight wools, silks, batistes, linens, muslins, or polyesters. The embroidery floss should be suitable to the weight and texture of the base fabric. You would not want to use a heavy floss on a lightweight fabric. Six-strand cotton embroidery floss is easy to work with and suits most fabrics. Silks, linens, perle cottons, rayons, wools, and metallic threads can be used effectively, too. DMC embroidery floss offers a wide selection of colors and produces a beautiful finished product. Remember that all thread (and floss) has a grain and "direction." You can feel it by holding the thread at one end and running your fingers down the thread. One direction will feel smoother than the other. The thread should be pulled through the fabric in the smooth direction. To find it, knot the end you cut as you pull the thread out of a skein or off a spool. This will usually be the right direction. If you have unusual tangling, you are probably working against the grain. Pull the thread out and knot the other end. Working with the grain will enable you to produce smooth stitches. (Never work with a doubled strand of floss; one strand will be pulled against the grain.)

The needle should be a sharp crewel, embroidery or darning needle. For most projects I prefer a number 8 crewel embroidery needle, although some people prefer a cotton darning needle. When working on a coarse or heavy fabric with a thick thread, such as perle cotton or with six-ply strands of floss, use a number 5 needle. On very fine fabric, such as a lightweight batiste, where the smocking is to be very delicate and only one or two-ply strands are used, a number 10 needle is a better choice. The needle should be one with which you feel comfortable working and one that suits the nature of the project.

Cutting Fabrics

In cutting fabric, you must allow extra fabric for the area to be smocked. The normal rule of thumb is a three-to-one ratio; that is, 3 inches (7.5 cm) of fabric for 1 inch of finished smocking. However, this ratio may need to be varied depending on the weight of fabric and the design or smocking stitches within the design. For example, if you use a lightweight fabric, such as batiste or silk, and the smocking design is very dense, the ratio may be increased to five or six to one. On the other hand, if the fabric is heavy and the design is open with diamonds, the ratio can be two to one.

Gathering Pleats

Now you must form uniform, evenly spaced pleats with rows of evenly spaced gathering threads. These threads can be worked through the fabric in a number of different methods.

If you are working with a printed fabric, such as dotted Swiss, stripes, or gingham, use the print itself as a guideline for the gathering threads. (See Figures 1-1, 1-2, and 1-3.) If you are working with a solid fabric, there are several other methods you can use.

One method is to lightly draw a grid on the wrong side of the fabric, using a ruler and pencil. Each line should be drawn ¼ inch (6 mm) apart. Then each corner can be picked up. (See Figure 1-3.) Another method is to place dressmaker's carbon paper be-

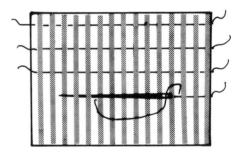

1-2 Gathering the pleats on striped fabric.

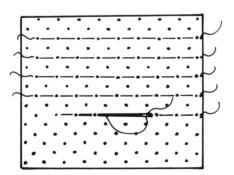

1-1 Gathering the pleats on dotted Swiss fabric.

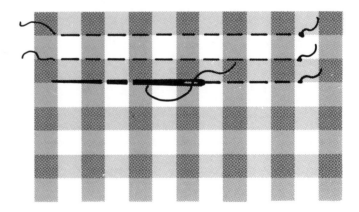

1-3 Gathering the pleats on gingham fabric.

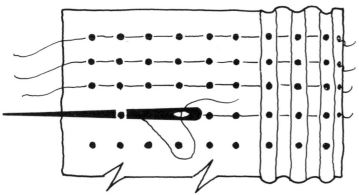

1-4 To gather pleats bring needle in one side of the printed dot and out the other.

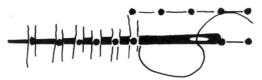

1-5 For faster results, pick up several dots at one time.

tween a ¼-inch piece of graph paper and the fabric. Mark each corner of the paper as a dot to be picked up.

A third method involves blue or yellow dot transfer sheets, available in notions departments. These are tissues consisting of evenly spaced dots. Yellow should be used for light color fabrics and blue for dark.

Transfer the appropriate number of rows of dots to the *wrong* side of the fabric. To do this, tape or pin the tissue to the fabric so that it does not move. Being careful not to rub, press firmly with a *warm, dry* iron. (Always pretest your fabric to make sure the dots will wash out later. If the dots bleed through the fabric they will be difficult to wash out. The solution may be to use a low heat setting. If the dots still do not wash out, place dressmaker's carbon paper between the tissue and fabric and mark the dots with the point of a knitting needle or some other blunt point.)

Once you have your dots on the fabric, you are ready to use them as a guide for pleating. Use a cotton darning needle that is long and thin. Firmly knot a length of contrasting color thread slightly longer than the width of the fabric. Heavy-duty quilting thread makes a good gathering thread. Take a backstitch on the right-hand side of the row to be pleated (left-hand for "lefties"). If you wish, rub the gathering thread with beeswax to prevent knots and breakage. Pick up each dot by going in one side of the dot and out the other.

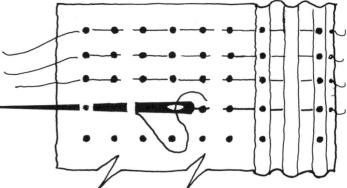

1-6 For a deeper pleat, pick up a space between two dots, skip a dot, and pick up the next dot. Use this method on thick fabrics.

(See Figures 1-4 and 1-5.) Once you get used to the motion, develop speed by picking up several dots on the needle before pulling the needle through and moving to the next series of dots.

Three-sixteenths-inch spacing is a standard spacing for pleats and rows of gathering threads. Keep in mind that it is the dots, not the size of the smocking stitches, that set the pleat size and distance between the rows of gathering threads. If you want a very fine smocked look for an infant's gown, for example, the 3/16-inch (7 mm) pleating will do very nicely. To create the delicate effect that is needed for a very fine, lightweight fabric, you may wish to smock with only two plies of embroidery floss, instead of the usual three plies. You would still use the 3/16-inch pleats. For heavy fabrics, on the other hand, deeper pleats are necessary. In this case, you would simply pick up a dot, then skip to the space between the next two dots. The Curved-Yoke Rain Jacket on page 119 was worked this way.

As discussed earlier, patterned fabrics, such as dotted Swiss, provide their own guidelines. You have only to pick up dots as if a transfer were being used. Use alternate rows of dots (as shown in Figure 1-6).

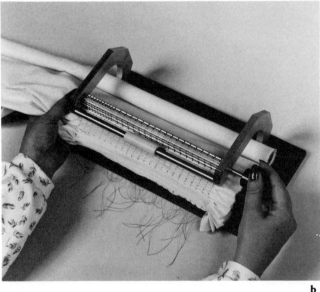

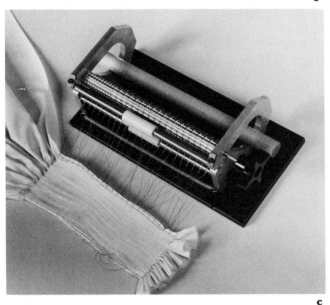

1-7 a, b, and c a) 24-Row Durand Pleater with bobbin rack and thread guide; b) fabric is rolled on a dowel and, with the turn of the handle, the fabric passes between the pleating rods and out the front; c) the pleated fabric ready to be smocked.

When pleating on stripes or plaids, mark horizontal straight rows on the wrong side of the fabric. If the vertical stripes are too wide for you to go in one side and out the other, mark dots in the middle of each stripe along the horizontal guidelines. For gingham fabrics, treat each lower right-hand corner as if it were a dot. (See Figure 1-3.) If a ⅛-inch (3 mm) gingham is used, go from one corner to the next.

For those who do a great deal of smocking, a smocking pleater may be a real blessing. (See Figure 1-7.) This 12-inch (25.4 cm) hand tool can pleat up to twenty-four rows with just the turn of a handle. Smocking pleaters are available through some needlework stores or can be ordered through the mail. (See Sources in the back of this book.) In a matter of minutes fabric can be rolled onto a dowel, passed through rollers onto as many as twenty-four needles, the gathering threads pulled through each pleat, and the fabric pressed into uniform, crisp pleats. The number of rows can be adjusted by simply removing some of the needles. You can pleat one to twenty-four rows at one time. (If your project requires more than twenty-four rows, simply run the fabric through a twenty-four row pleater. Leave threads long enough so that the fabric can be spread flat. Use tailor chalk to mark a guideline ¾ inch (20 mm) below the last row.

Pleat the additional rows, following the chalk guideline —see Figure 1-8—on the first row. Pull the fabric into tight pleats. Run a gathering thread between the two pleated areas by hand—See Figure 1-9. This is necessary to align the pleats in the two areas.) Most light- to medium- weight fabrics may be pleated on the pleater.

Regardless of which pleating method you have used, after all the gathering threads have been run through the fabric, pull the fabric into tight pleats.

Stretch the fabric lengthwise to straighten out the pleats, and hold a steam iron approximately ½ inch (1.27 cm) over the fabric to set them. (It is not necessary to steam the pleats if a pleater has been used.) After the fabric cools, spread the pleats so that the gathering threads are barely visible. Tie the ends of the gathering threads, two rows together, with an overhand knot. (See Figure 1-10.)

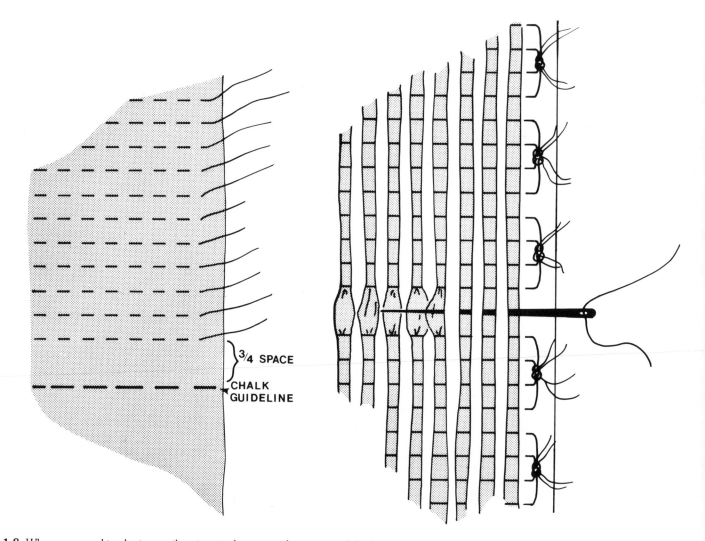

1-8 When you need to pleat more than twenty-four rows, draw in a guideline ¾ inch below the last row.

1-9 After you have pleated the additional rows, hand pleat the row you marked as a guideline.

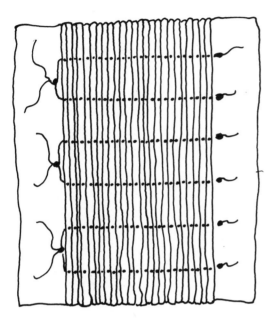

1-10 Tie the ends of two threads together to hold the gathered pleats in place.

Smocking

Now that your pleats are set, you are ready to start smocking. Most smocking stitches are a variation of the basic backstitch done through pleats. (See Figure 1-11.) They are simply embroidery stitches adapted to working across pleats. Smocking stitches are referred to by different names, by different people, but the basic techniques involved are the same. The Stitch Glossary starting on page 16 will show you how to make all the major stitches, but there are a few rules which must be followed regardless of which stitch you use.

Basic Rules

- Always hold the needle parallel to the gathering threads (exception: the Raised Chain and variations of the Feather stitch).
- Pick up one-third the depth of each pleat (Figure 1-12) and go through one pleat at a time. (exception: the Van Dyke, Feather, Herringbone, and Honeycomb stitches and there may be other

1-11 A basic backstitch.

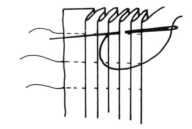

1-12 Pick up one-third of the depth of each pleat.

times when this rule might be modified). As the thread comes out of the pleat, pull gently, but firmly.

- Keep tension consistent in order for the stitches to look smooth and neat.
- Leave about three pleats or ⅝ inch (1.5 cm) on each side of the smocking for your seam allowance. The beginning and ending pleats of the smocking should be caught in the seam.

Starting and Ending

Work with three-ply lengths of embroidery floss, about 20 to 22 inches (50.8 cm to 55.9 cm) long. Knot one end firmly. Bring needle up on the left-hand side of the first pleat and take a stitch through the second pleat. (See Figure 1-13.)

1-14 Ending a row of smocking.

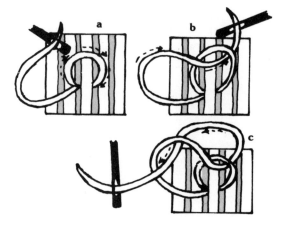

1-15 a, b, and c Alternate ways to end a row of smocking.

1-13 Start a row of smocking.

To end a row, take the needle to the back on the right-hand side of the last pleat. Secure with two back-stitches through the back of the last pleat (see Figure 1-14) or make a loop and knot as illustrated. (See Figures 1-15a, b, and c.)

If the thread is not long enough to complete a row, you will need to end in the middle of a row. To do so, simply carry the thread to the back of the fabric with the completion of a straight stitch (Cable, Stem, or Outline), and make a backstitch knot in the last pleat worked (See Figures 1-16a, b, and c.) Begin the new thread by taking a backstitch in that same pleat and bring the needle up in the valley on the left side of the pleat. Continue to smock the rest of the row.

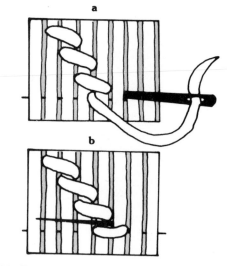

1-16 a and b Ending in the middle of the row.

Positioning the Pleats

The pleats are positioned so that they are close together, but not so close as to make it difficult to pick up the pleats as you smock. Hold the fabric between the forefinger and the middle finger, and between the thumb and the ring finger. (See Figure 1-17.) Use the thumb to spread the pleats apart as you smock. The smocking will expand to the finished width after the gathering threads are removed, if enough fabric has been allowed for the size and if you do not stitch more than one-third into the pleat.

1-17 How to hold the pleats as you smock.

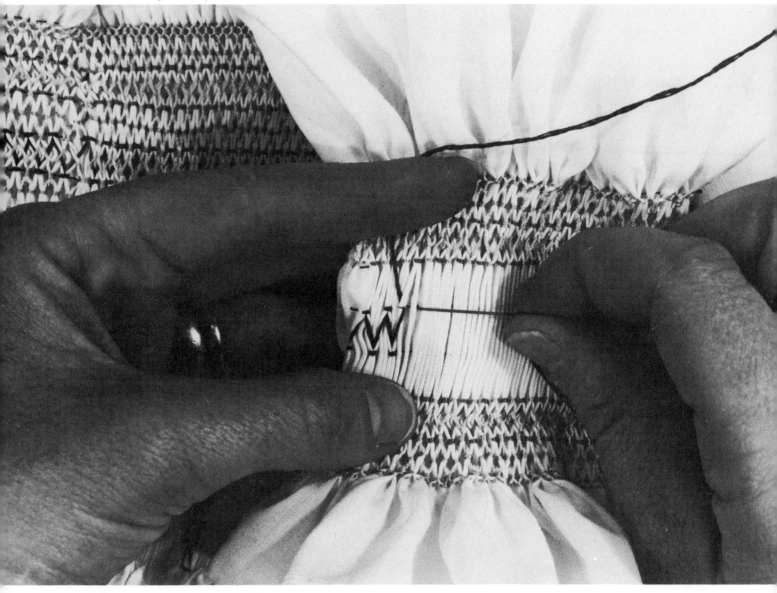

Stitch Glossary

In the following diagrams this symbol ○ will illustrate where the needle has gone through the pleats. A white bar represents a pleat and a gray bar represents a valley between pleats. It is impossible to diagram all the variations of the stitches. However, the following stitches are some of the most common variations.

About Straight Stitches

This family of stitches, which includes Cable, Outline, Stem, Chain, and Raised Chain, are generally worked straight across the pleats following the gathering threads. Straight stitches provide the control necessary, for example around a neckline or cuff on a blouse. Two rows worked closely together at the top or bottom of the smocking will hold gathers firmly in place. These stitches should not be used where a loose flare is needed, such as at the bottom of a yoke. Many designs are balanced by using these stitches to add color in a small area, and there may be times when these stitches can be curved to form shapes in free-form smocking designs.

When working a straight stitch, the needle passes through one pleat at a time, about a needle's width above or below the gathering thread. (See Figure.) This will help prevent catching the thread and making it difficult to pull out. The symbol ○ indicates the points where the needle goes through each pleat. Remember to take only one-third the depth of the pleat.

CABLE STITCH
Cable, considered to be "the basic stitch," has many uses. Use it to align pleats, to control fullness around necklines, and to separate sections of a design. To make a row of Cable stitches, pick up one pleat at a time, alternating the thread above the needle, and then below, as shown in Figure A. An "up" Cable is made with the thread held above the needle. A "down" Cable is made with the thread held below the needle. (See Figure B.)

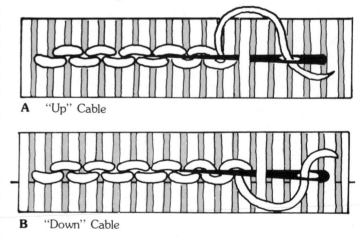

A "Up" Cable

B "Down" Cable

Cables can be stacked to form pyramids and squares. In designs where there are blank areas, where the pleats need to be held after the gathering threads have been pulled out, Cable stitches should be used to backsmock across the back of the pleats. (See page 30.)

OUTLINE STITCH
The Outline stitch is worked across the pleats in much the same way as the Cable, but the thread is *always*

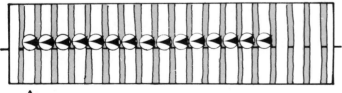

A

Straight Stitch
◗ illustrates the position at which the needle has passed through the pleat, a needle width above the gathering thread.

held above the needle. For this stitch, consistent tension, the depth with which you take each pleat, and the position at which you pick up each pleat are most important. (See Figure.) This stitch is useful for adding accent color to a design.

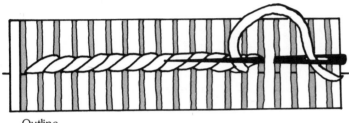

Outline

STEM STITCH

The Stem is worked the same way as the Outline stitch, but the thread is always held below the needle. (See Figure.)

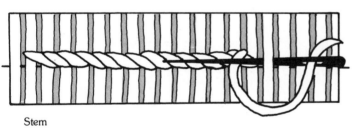

Stem

CHAIN STITCH

The Chain stitch is worked from right to left. Start the Chain stitch by bringing the needle up through a valley. Insert the needle through the first pleat, keep-

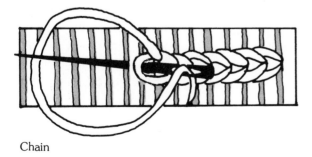

Chain

ing the thread under the needle to form a large loop. Draw the thread so that a small loop is formed. Insert the needle through the loop and the next pleat, keeping the thread under the needle. (See Figure.) Keep loops to the same side with consistent tension.

The Chain stitch can be worked into curves to outline and form various shapes.

RAISED CHAIN STITCH

The Raised Chain is worked from right to left. It is similar to the Chain, but with the Raised Chain the needle is inserted into the same pleat twice. Insert the needle through the pleat from the left side to the right side. (It may be easier to turn the pleats horizontally.) Draw the thread through the pleat. Insert the needle from the right side to the left side, keeping the thread under the needle. (See Figures A and B.)

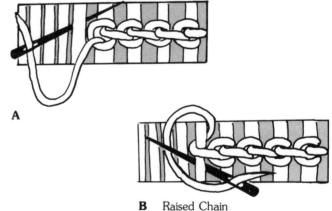

A

B   Raised Chain

About Zigzag Stitches

This family of stitches includes the Trellis, Chevron, Van Dyke, Surface Honeycomb, Honeycomb, and Herringbone stitches. These stitches are worked in the areas between rows of gathering threads and have more elasticity than do the Straight stitches. They can be worked into many shapes—waves, diamonds, chevron designs, lattices, and pyramids. They provide a good background area for accent Fill-In stitches. The height of these stitches can be varied according to the demands of the design.

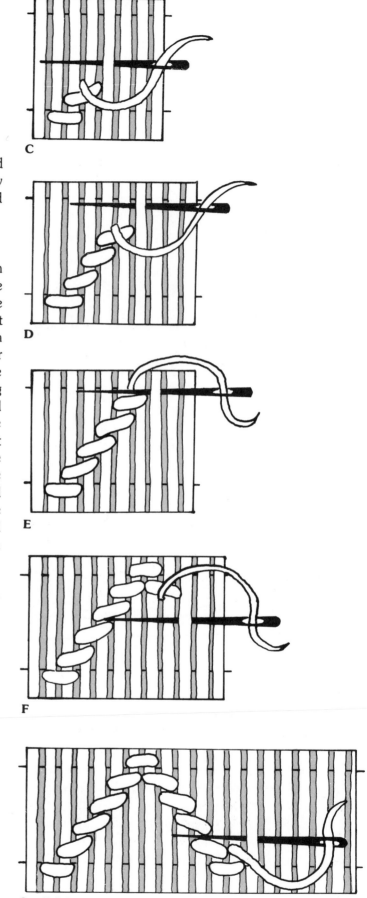

A general rule for Zigzag stitches is to keep thread below the needle for the bottom stitch, thread below when going up, thread above for the top stitch, and thread above to go down.

FULL-SPACE TRELLIS

Start with a bottom point by bringing the needle up on the left side of the first pleat. Take a stitch through the next pleat at the same level, with the thread below the needle. Take the next stitch through the next pleat one-quarter the distance between the previous stitch and the next row of gathering threads. Repeat for one-half the distance, then three-quarters, etc. Make sure the thread always follows the needle. When going up, hold the thread below the needle. The process will continue until the Trellis is the desired height. Make the top point by taking a stitch through the next pleat at the same level as the last stitch. Now work down the other side of the Trellis. Hold the thread above the needle while you are making the top of the Trellis and while the stitches are worked down the side of the Trellis. Work each stitch at one-quarter intervals until you reach the bottom point. (See Figures A through G.)

This stitch can be worked at intervals of one-half, one-third, one-fifth, one-sixth, etc., and built to various heights.

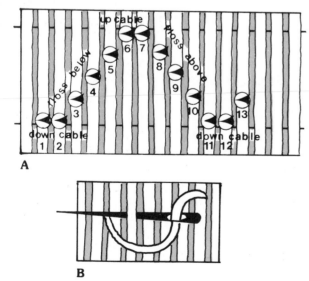

A

B

F

G   Full-Space Trellis

18

HALF-SPACE TRELLIS

This stitch is worked exactly like the Full-Space Trellis, except that when you get to the halfway point between the two gathering threads, you make an "up," or top Cable and start down the other side of the trellis. (See Figures A and B.) Note the position of ○ in B, indicating the point where the needle was inserted through the pleat.

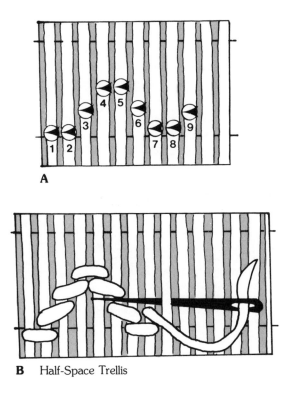

A

B   Half-Space Trellis

ZIGZAG TRELLIS

It is not necessary to make the Trellis symmetrical. By varying the heights of each side, you can create a diagonal zigzag. In the Figure a Half-Space Trellis is worked up one side, then a one-and-one-half-space Trellis is worked down the second side. Spacing of each stitch, in this case, is at one-quarter-space intervals between the gathering threads. You can achieve the same affect if you space each stitch at another interval, such as one-half, one-third, one-fifth. You will find this concept interesting to work into a design.

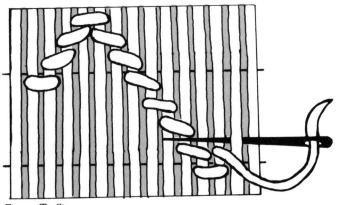

Zigzag Trellis

CHEVRON STITCH

The Chevron is a variation of a Straight Cable. To make the stitch, first work a "down" Cable on the gathering line, and then an "up" Cable either one-half space between the gathering lines or on the next gathering line. Again, the height may vary and one row may cross over another. (See Figures A and B.)

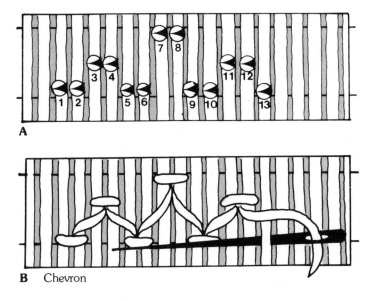

A

B   Chevron

CHEVRON DIAMOND

These are two rows of Chevrons worked opposite each other to form diamonds. Two pleats remain in the center of the diamond. (See Figure.)

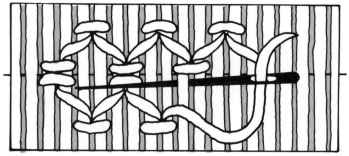

Chevron Diamond

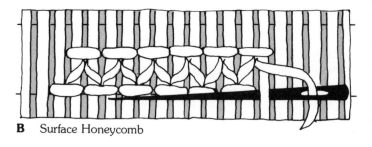

B Surface Honeycomb

CROSSOVER CHEVRON

Work one row of Full-Space Chevrons and then cross over it with a row of half-space Chevrons. (See Figure.)

SURFACE HONEYCOMB DIAMOND

These are formed by working two or more rows of Surface Honeycomb opposite to each other. (See Figure.) Unlike the Chevron Diamond, however, there will be no pleat in the middle of the diamond. The Surface Honeycomb Diamond is not as elastic as the Chevron Diamond.

Crossover Chevron

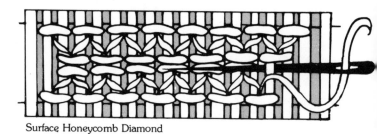

Surface Honeycomb Diamond

SURFACE HONEYCOMB

This stitch is similar to the Chevron, except that two stitches are taken in the same pleat. In other words, the same pleat is stitched twice. In Figure 1-41 you can see the point at which the needle is inserted through the pleat. (See Figures A and B.)

HONEYCOMB

Since the Honeycomb is a very elastic stitch, it requires less fabric. For most designs 3 inches (7.5 cm) of fabric is needed for 1 inch (2.5 cm) of finished smocking. If Honeycomb is the dominant stitch, then only 2 or 2½ inches (5 or 6.4 cm) of fabric is needed for 1 inch of finished smocking.

Begin by coming up on the left side of the first pleat slightly above the second gathering thread from the top. Insert the needle through two pleats at once and

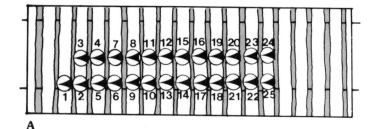

A

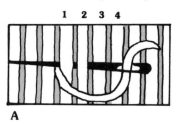

A

draw the thread through the pleats. Insert the needle into the valley between the second and third pleats to the back of work. (See Figures A and B.) Bring the

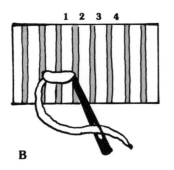

B

needle from the back up through the valley between the first and second pleats slightly below the first gathering thread. Insert the needle through the second and third pleats. Push the needle to the back between the third and fourth pleats at the same level as the previous stitch. (See Figures C and D.) Insert the needle from the back to the front through the valley between the second and third pleats, slightly above the second

gathering thread. Insert the needle through the third and fourth pleats, then back through the valley between the fourth and fifth pleats. Continue the row in this manner. (See Figure E.) Work a second row between the third and fourth gathering threads.

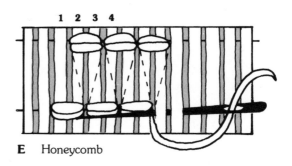

E Honeycomb

HERRINGBONE

The Herringbone stitch creates an interesting effect as the threads cross over each other. When two rows are worked together the pleats between form a honeycomb shape.

Pass the needle through two pleats at once; then an old pleat and a new one. The stitch moves from the left to the right. (See Figure.)

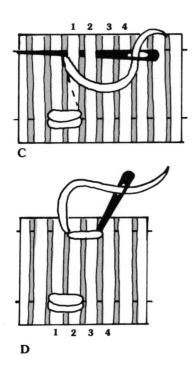

C

D

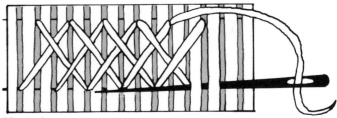

Herringbone

DOUBLE HERRINGBONE

This stitch is a variation of the Herringbone. An extra stitch is taken at the top and the bottom of the stitch. The pleats are held tighter than with the Herringbone. (See Figure.) The Double Herringbone is beautiful when worked in a zigzag, similar to the Van Dyke Zigzag.

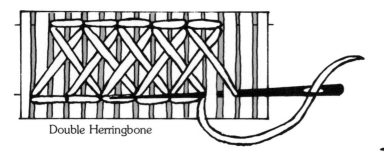
Double Herringbone

points at which you insert the needle through the pleats will be at half-space intervals between the gathering threads. (See Figure.) Always keep the thread above the needle when moving down and below the needle when moving up.

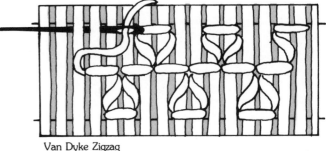
Van Dyke Zigzag

STRAIGHT VAN DYKE

This stitch is worked right to left. Start out by bringing the needle up through the valley on the right side of the first pleat. Insert the needle through two pleats. Then insert the needle back through the same two pleats with the thread above the needle. Draw the thread through the pleats. Spacing either at a full-space or a half-space interval (halfway between the next row of gathering threads), insert the needle through an old pleat and a new pleat. Then insert the needle through the same two pleats with the thread held below the needle. (See A and B.)

FREEFORM FEATHER STITCH

The Feather stitch is one of the oldest smocking stitches. It is found on many old English smocks. The stitch is worked from right to left and is fairly elastic. Bring the needle up through the valley on the right side of the first pleat slightly below the gathering thread. Insert the needle through two pleats with the thread held under the needle. Draw the thread through the pleats to form a loop. Insert the needle

A   Half-Space Van Dyke

B   Full-Space Van Dyke

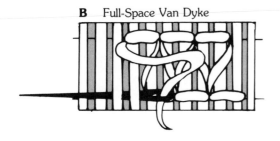

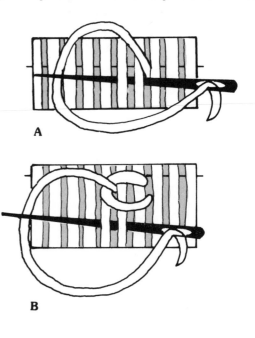

A

B

VAN DYKE ZIGZAG

Work the Zigzag the same way as you would a Straight Van Dyke stitch except for one major difference. The

through two pleats, an old pleat and a new one, with the thread held under the needle. Insert the needle through two pleats, slightly below the gathering thread, with the thread under the needle. Then insert the needle through two pleats two-thirds between the gathering threads. This will create a larger loop and will begin to give the effect of a cloudlike shape. Insert the needle through two pleats slightly below the gathering thread. (See Figures A through E.)

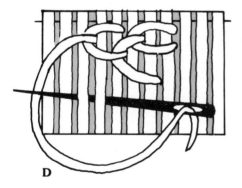

C

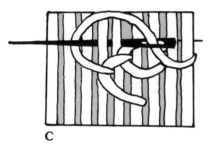

D

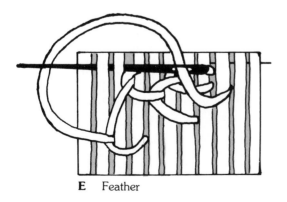

E   Feather

STRAIGHT FEATHER STITCH

Begin by bringing the needle through the valley on the right side of the first pleat. Insert the needle through two pleats at a 45-degree angle to the gathering thread. Make each stitch with the needle held at the same angle. (See Figure.)

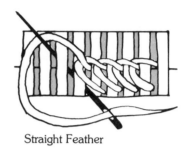

Straight Feather

ALTERNATING FEATHER STITCH

Make this stitch by inserting the needle at a 45-degree angle above the gathering thread, then below the gathering thread. (See Figure.)

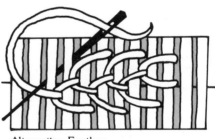

Alternating Feather

BROAD FEATHER STITCH

Work this stitch with the needle parallel to the gathering thread. This is a good stitch to use when you want to add a fill-in color between two rows of gathering threads. (See Figure.)

A   Broad Feather

About Accent Stitches

Flowerette, Seed stitch, Satin stitch, French Knot, Boullion Rose, and Turkey Work are all accent stitches. These stitches are used to introduce detail to a design. Depending on how they are used, they can emphasize a theme or give detail and produce rhyme in a design. These simple stitches are a designer's tool to creating interesting effects in any design. A contrasting or complementary color can be added to a design with one of these stitches.

Accent stitches are usually added to a design after the gathering threads have been removed. Many of these stitches can be used on collars of yokes to add the final touch. These accent stitches have no elasticity.

SINGLE FLOWERETTE

This stitch is simply a group of four Cables worked to form a flower. It is worked from left to right. Begin with a "down" Cable. Bring the needle up through the valley on the left side of the first pleat. Insert the needle through the second pleat with the thread held below the needle. Insert the needle through the third pleat with the thread held above the needle. Next, insert the needle through the fourth pleat with the thread held above the needle. Finally, push the needle to the back through the valley between the first and second pleats. Secure thread with a backstitch. (See A through D.)

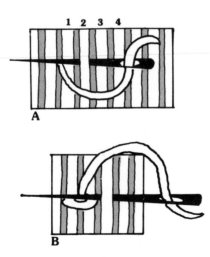

A

B

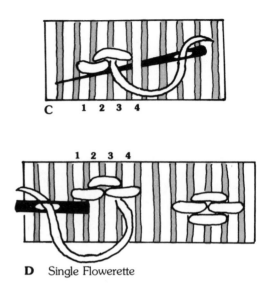

C   1 2 3 4

D   Single Flowerette

SEED STITCH

This is the smallest of the accent stitches. To make it, begin with the needle coming up on the left side of the first pleat. Insert the needle through the first and second pleats at the same time. Draw the thread through the pleats. Push the needle to the back of the fabric through the valley on the right side of the second pleat. (See Figure.) Secure thread with a backstitch.

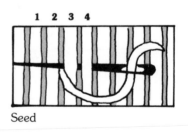

Seed

DOUBLE FLOWERETTE

A group of six Cables worked to form a flower. Work a "down" Cable, then an "up" Cable. Push the needle through the fourth, third, second, and first pleats. Insert the needle through the second pleat with the thread held above the needle. Then insert the needle through the third pleat with the thread held below the needle. End by pushing the needle to the back through the valley on the right side of the fourth pleat. Secure thread with a backstitch. (See Figures A through C.)

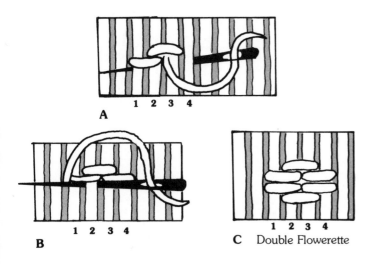

A

B

C Double Flowerette

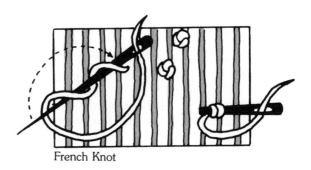

French Knot

SATIN STITCH

This is similar to the Seed stitch, but larger. It can be used to form solid bars of color. Begin by coming up through the valley on the left side of the first pleat. Insert the needle through two pleats at once. Work as many stitches as is required to fill a space. Three or four pleats may be used instead of two. (See Figure.) The stitch will be prettier if you pick up the whole pleat. Do not pull too tightly.

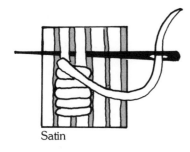

Satin

FRENCH KNOT

The French Knot is a simple knotted stitch used to form flower centers and to add color accents. Bring the needle up through the peak of a pleat. Wind the thread over the needle two, three, or more times, depending upon the size of the knot needed. Insert the needle close to where it came out. Draw the needle to the wrong side and secure with a backstitch through two pleats. (See Figure.)

BOULLION STITCH

This stitch is a coil of thread made by taking a back-stitch, twisting the thread around the needle several times, and pulling the thread through the coil. Bring the needle up through the peak of a pleat. Then insert the needle through the peak of a second pleat and up at the same place as before. Wind the thread over the needle several times—enough to fill the space for the length of the stitch. Hold the "wind" with the left hand, while pulling the thread through the pleats.

BOULLION ROSE

A Boullion Rose is formed by working two or three coils of the Boullion stitch next to each other. The center coil is usually a deeper shape than the two on the outside. Work three to form a rosebud and use daisy loops for leaves. (See Figure.)

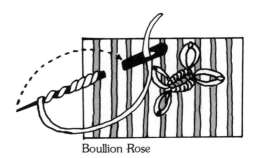

Boullion Rose

TURKEY WORK

This stitch is really just a looped Cable. After the stitch is worked, the threads are cut and fluffed. These stitches may be used to make looped flowers, plants, or furry animals. Insert the needle through the first pleat, leaving a tail of thread. Next, insert the needle through the second pleat. Draw the thread, being careful not to pull too tightly. Insert the needle through the third pleat, leaving a loop of thread. Then insert the needle through the fourth pleat, drawing the thread all the way through the pleat. Continue in this manner. Trim the threads of the loops and fluff with the blunt end of the needle. (See Figures A through F.)

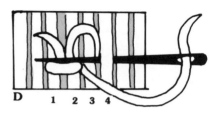

D 1 2 3 4

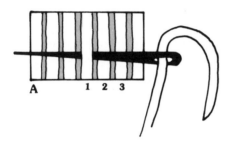

A 1 2 3

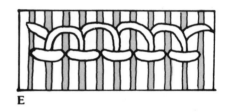

E

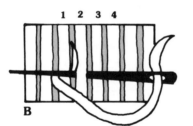

1 2 3 4

B

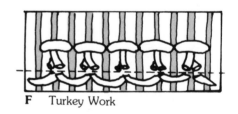

F Turkey Work

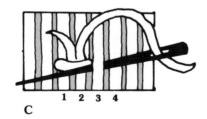

1 2 3 4

C

About Combinations and Variations of Stitches

Once you have mastered the basic stitches, there are an endless number of variations and combinations you may use in a design. The following stitches represent only a few possibilities.

OUTLINE–STEM STITCH
Outlines opposite Stems make a mock chain or a braid. (See Figure.)

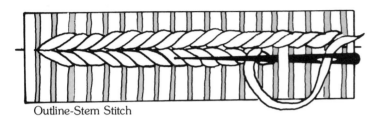

Outline-Stem Stitch

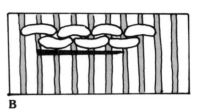

B

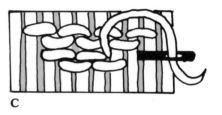

C

STACKED CABLE STITCH
Parallel rows of Cables will create squares as in the first and second rows in the Figure. The second and third rows show the pyramid effect achieved when a parallel row is done as a mirror image of the first.

D   Cable Pyramid

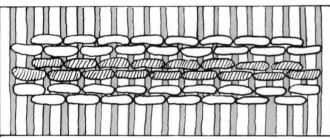

Stacked Cable Stitch

CABLE PYRAMID
Work a base row of Cables. Push needle to back. Turn work upside down. Bring the needle up in a valley. Complete the row. Push the needle to the back. Begin again and continue until the pyramid is built. (See Figures A through D.)

HALF-SPACE CHEVRON CABLE
Work a complete Chevron stitch, but, before making the second Chevron, make an "up" Cable and a "down" Cable, then complete the second Chevron. (See Figure.) Extra Cable stitches are often worked between a Zigzag stitch. You will find many variations throughout this text.

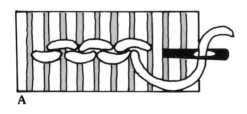

A

Half-Space Chevron Cable

CROSSOVER CHEVRON CABLE

The basic stitches can be worked together to form a stitch combination such as Chevron Cable. Rows may be worked over each other to form crossover rows. (See Figures A and B.)

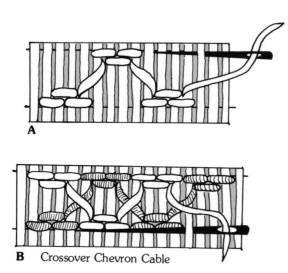

A

B Crossover Chevron Cable

CABLE WITH ALTERNATING CABLE

Work a base row of Cables, then alternate three Cables on each side of the base row. (See Figure.)

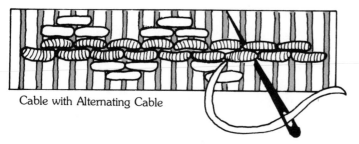

Cable with Alternating Cable

LAZY DAISY

Bring the needle through the peak of the first pleat. Insert the needle close to where the needle came up, then out through the peak of another pleat with the thread under the needle. Then, push the needle to the back of the fabric through the side of the pleat.

Begin the next loop close to the point where the first loop began. Finish by working a French Knot in the center of the loops. (See Figures A through C.)

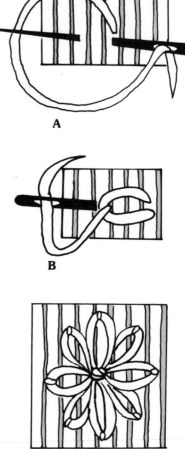

A

B

C Lazy Daisy

FLOWERETTE POINT

This technique can be used on an "up" or "down" point of any of the Zigzag stitches where the Flowerette is to be done in the same color as the stitch. Work the stitch to an "up" point. Push the needle through *three* pleats, with the thread held below the needle. (See Figure A.) Push the needle through the second pleat with thread held below the needle to make a "down" Cable. (See Figure B.) Push the needle through the

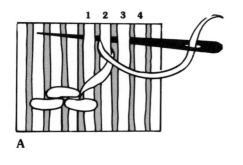

A

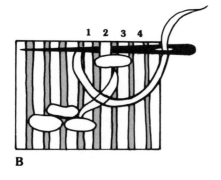

B

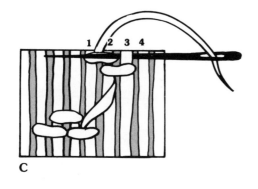

C

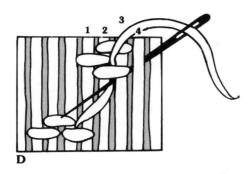

D

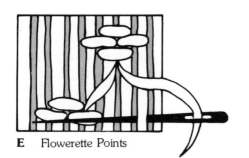

E   Flowerette Points

third pleat with thread held above the needle to make an "up" Cable. (See C.) Push the needle through the fourth and third pleats, coming out just under the first Cable. This will complete the Flowerette. (See Figures A and E.)

BOULLION LOOP

You can use a cluster of this variation on the Boullion stitch to form an accent flower. Bring the needle up through the peak of a pleat. Pass the needle through the same pleat just above the thread. Then wind the thread around the needle fifteen or more times. Hold the coil with the left thumb, while pulling the needle and thread through the coil. Pull tightly and shape coil into a loop. Push needle through the peak of the pleat close to the base of the loop. Secure thread in the back of the pleat. Tack loop into place the same as you would for a Lazy Daisy Loop. (See Figures A through C.)

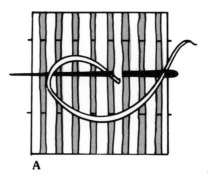

A

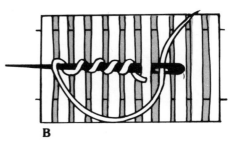

B

C   Boullion Loop

FILL-IN STITCHES

Any accent or embroidery stitch can be used as a Fill-In stitch within a design. This technique may affect a design dramatically. These stitches are worked into the design after the background has been completed. Since these stitches have very little elasticity, care must be taken so that the elasticity of the total design will not

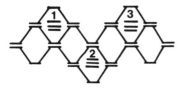

A

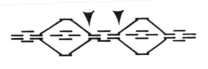

B

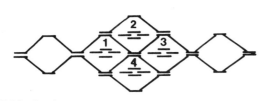

C   Fill-In Stitch

be affected. Position the stitches so that the threads are more or less vertical with the pleats. If the thread passes behind more than four pleats, backsmock from one placement to the next. Before moving from one position to the next, make a backstitch behind the stitch so that it will not become misshapen when the smocking is blocked. If there is a group of stitches, work in a circular manner and tie each group separately. There are many examples of this use of stitch throughout the book.

About Backsmocking

This technique is simply a matter of working the Cable or Trellis stitch on the wrong side of the fabric. These stitches hold pleats in place in designs where there are a lot of open spaces or where a lot of freeform embroidery is used. In addition to holding the pleats, the stitches create a soft "shadow" in the pleats.

Always use the same color thread as the fabric. In some designs Cable stitches may work better than Trellis, or vice versa. You will have to determine which stitch and how many stitches to make for yourself.

Backsmocking is useful in areas where more support is needed, such as around a cuff or neckline or top of a sundress. Backsmocking will balance the tension on both sides of the fabric so that a ruffle will stand up straight rather than curl over. Elastic thread can be used in cases where more control is needed.

About Freeform Smocking

Freeform smocking is a creative use of smocking techniques to create "smocked pictures." Start by pulling the pleats together and lightly sketching the general areas that will be filled in with stitches. Figure 1-18 shows the Farm Scene. Outline the apple tree with Outline stitch. Work apples in Cable stitch, then fill in with Surface Honeycomb. Do the wheat fields and then the sun in rows of Outline stitches. The farm house is Stacked Cables, with windows in Satin stitch.

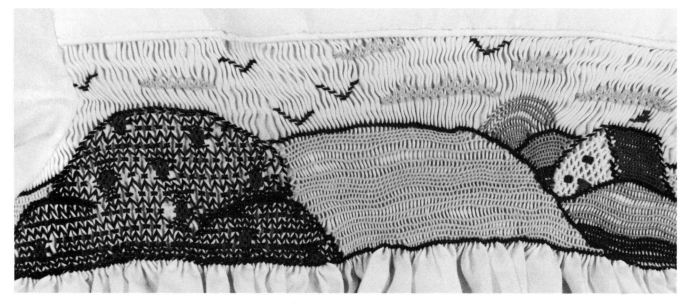

1-18 The Farm Scene is an example of freeform smocking.

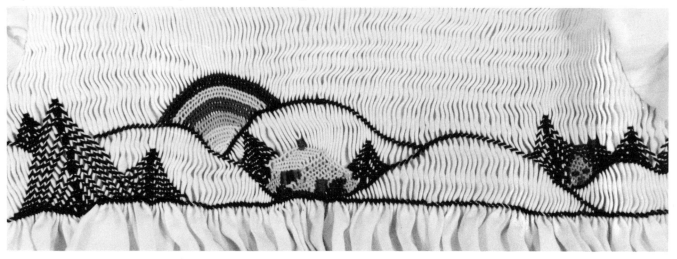

1-19 Rainbow Hill is a beautiful freeform smocking design. A little girl's dressing utilizing this design can be found on page 86.

For the clouds use the Feather stitch and for the birds use Trellis. Do all backsmocking in Cable.

Figure 1-19 shows Rainbow Hill. For this design do the hills and rainbow in Outline stitch, the pine trees in Stacked Trellis, and the houses in Stacked Cable. The roof is Outline stitch and the windows are Satin stitch. Do all the backsmocking in Cable.

Figure 1-20 shows Mountain Valley. For the road use the Feather stitch. The house is Stacked Cable, the roof is Outline, and the windows are Satin stitch. Use Stacked Trellis for the firs and fill in mountains with Outline and Honeycomb stitches. Do Feather Stitching for the road. For trees use Satin stitch for the trunk and Van Dyke for the leaves. Work Outline stitches around the outside. The sun too is Outline stitches, flowers are French Knots, and all backsmocking is Cable.

1-20 Another lovely freeform design—Mountain Valley.

It is not necessary to follow any particular order of working stitches. The amount of fabric needed with freeform smocking is more or less the same as for regular smocking. If the design is heavily worked, more fabric is needed. Backsmocking is important in areas where there is no smocking on the front.

Freeform smocking can be used on the front of children's garments, as inserts in pillows, or can be framed with a fabric matting around the outside. It is the most creative form of smocking.

Blocking

- After you have completed the design, remove the gathering threads. Then pin the smocked piece, face down, to an ironing board, stretching if necessary until it equals the desired finished width. (See Figure 1-21.) Block the piece by holding a steam iron about 1 inch (2.5 cm) over the work. Do not press.
- Round yokes are blocked after the placket and bias neck binding are stitched into place. Lay the dress or blouse flat so that the yoke can be spread into a circle. Block by holding the steam iron over the smocked area. It is easier to do this if the side seams are not stitched. Remember to make sure your iron is clean!

1-21 Blocking the smocked piece.

Things to Keep in Mind

- As in kitting, the tension of smocking stitches will vary with each individual. Just remember this: pull each stitch just until it is snug.
- The tension of the smocking stitches, the fabric worked on, the number of plies of floss, and the spaces left unworked between the rows of smocking all contribute to the finished width and elasticity of the smocking.
- Very fine, closely spaced smocking on thin fabric will not expand as much as will well-spaced smocking done with more strands of threads on heavier fabrics. Therefore, it is important to consider these factors when planning your work.
- Tight, nonelastic smocking can be due to several things: the smocking threads may have been pulled so tightly that the pleats are riveted together; too many rows of stitches may have been crammed into the design; the stitches may be too deep in each pleat (deeper than one-third).
- To avoid a situation where the smocked area does not expand across the required finished area, the ratio of fabric to required finished area can be predetermined. Medium- or heavyweight fabrics with an open design will expand more than a lightweight fabric with a heavy design and a lot of Fill-In stitches. The ratio of fabric to required finished area is three to one for medium- to heavyweight fabric with an open design; four (or five) to one for lightweight fabrics with many close rows and/or a lot of Fill-In stitches.
- Remember that the appearance or feeling of the design is affected by the weight of the fabric. For a very fine, lacy effect on infant gowns and other delicate apparel, use one-ply strands of floss on lightweight fabrics. But, for a solid, sturdy effect, use medium- to heavyweight fabric with heavier floss. On very heavy fabric, you will need a deeper pleat. (Refer to Gathering Pleats on page 9.)
- In designs where a lot of white or open space is used, backsmock every ½ inch (1.27 cm) on the reverse side using the Cable stitch to hold the pleats. Always work with a thread the same color as the fabric.

When Things Go Wrong

- Check your stitches frequently and learn to recognize mistakes. Be prepared to pull out incorrect or poorly done stitches when necessary.
- The worst thing is knowing your design has not worked and not knowing why. You must learn to look at your work with a critical eye as you are working the smocking stitches, as well as when you finish.
- Do not continue steadfastly smocking with planned colors and stitches when in your heart you know they are not turning out quite right. A slight alteration could make all the difference—a touch of color here or lighter shades on one side of the design, or a row of Outline or Cable there.
- When all is not going well, perhaps you should put the work away for a few hours or days and return with a fresh eye.

Reading Design Graphs

For each project in Part 3, the pattern has been illustrated on a design graph. By following it you can reproduce the spacing and color scheme. In most cases the graph will only show a portion of the design, which is repeated across the full smocked area.

Study the sample Design Graph in Figure 1-22. It will familiarize you with the codes you will be seeing in Part 3. For example, each numbered heavy horizontal line represents a gathering thread, while each vertical line represents a pleat. A slash across a line shows the interval between the rows of gathering threads where the needle goes through a pleat (half-space, quarter-space, etc.) Base Rows are indicated with arrows. These should be worked first and used as reference points for the adjacent rows. Colors are indicated by letters which follow the name of the stitch.

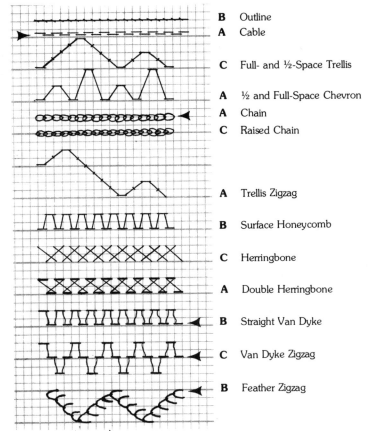

B	Outline
A	Cable
C	Full- and ½-Space Trellis
A	½ and Full-Space Chevron
A	Chain
C	Raised Chain
A	Trellis Zigzag
B	Surface Honeycomb
C	Herringbone
A	Double Herringbone
B	Straight Van Dyke
C	Van Dyke Zigzag
B	Feather Zigzag

Thread
DMC embroidery floss

Colors
A Red
B Blue
C Yellow

Example
On Row 1 do the Outline stitch in pink floss
On Row 5 do Raised Chain stitches in red floss

1-22 Reading a Design Graph.

PART TWO

Creating the Total Projects

Now that you have learned the basic smocking technique, you are ready to begin to plan a smocking project. Any of the projects in Part 3 could be tackled, although some are more difficult than others. It is always best to begin with a simple one which you can complete in a few hours. Pillows or Christmas ornaments are good for starter projects and there are two such starter projects at the end of this Part 2.

Before you begin a project, read Part 2 carefully. The information in it will be invaluable to you, whether you are making one of the projects in the book or designing your own from scratch.

Decorative Versus Functional Smocking

Before you begin any project you must plan it in your mind, and, the very first question you must ask yourself (other than "What do I want to make?") is "How do I want to utilize the smocking?"

There are essentially two ways to incorporate smocking into a garment. For one, you may insert the smocking as a decorative insert within the garment, and such an insert can be worked into a garment in a variety of different ways. In Part 3 you will find projects entitled Three Sundresses, Two Little Girls' Blouses, Father and Son Cherokee Shirts, Brother and Sister Jackets, and Curved-Yoke and Rain Jacket. These are good examples of decorative smocking. Once you have sewn the insert into the adjacent fabric, the remaining construction of the garment is basically the same as it would have been without this change.

In the second form smocking has a functional role in the construction of the garment, as well as a decorative one. Smocking can control and give shape to areas where the fullness of the fabric needs to be held close to the body. You can use it in any area where elasticity would normally be necessary. If you use smocking in this way, more fabric is required and the basic construction is altered. The sundress with the smocked bodice on page 81, the Flower-Girl and Mother-of-the-Bride Gowns, the Three Evening-Out Dresses, the China-Silk Peasant Blouse, Two Sisters' Nightgowns, Hooded Caftan, Little Girl's "Rainbow Hill" Dress, Little Girl's Pinafore and Bonnet, Bishop Dress, and Baby's Christening Gown are all excellent examples of projects where smocking plays a functional role.

Materials

Once you have an idea of what type of project you want to make and how smocking will be incorporated into the garment, you must choose a fabric. Consider color, texture, and washability of the fabric. It can be a good-quality cotton or cotton blend, wool, silk, batiste, linen, muslin, or polyester. Test the fabric to see how well it will pleat by creasing little pleats with your fingers. Some fabrics are "spongy" and pleats pop out once the gathering threads are pulled out. This will not create the same effect as crisp pleats. Consider the thickness of the fabric. Make sure it will suit your project. You would not want a thick broadcloth for a baby's gown or a fine wedding dress.

The color of the fabric has a great effect on the total design. Place different colors of floss on the fabric to see what combinations will look good against that background. The smocking design will show up best against a solid background. However, prints are fun to work with.

When you have chosen a fabric, you must select a good-quality thread. Six-ply cotton embroidery floss will work in most projects, but silk, linen, perle cotton, rayon, wool, and metallic threads can also be used. Your most important decision, at this point, once you've decided on what type of thread to use, will be colors. Read the section on Color and Design for some guidelines in choosing the color of threads.

Another very important consideration is pattern. There are a number of basic commercial patterns that have been designed for smocking. These are available in notion and needlework departments, or refer to Sources in the back of this book. If you cannot find one to meet the needs of your project, you can adapt a standard commercial pattern by following a few simple steps. Refer to the section on Construction for more details.

If you are planning a decorative insert, a basic shirtwaist pattern might work nicely. However, if you are planning for the smocking to have a functional purpose, select a pattern that has gathers, tucks, pleats, or shirring. Usually, you will need the same amount of fabric as is called for on the pattern, unless the pattern only has a small amount of gathers, tucks, pleats, or shirring. If you use an insert, the general rule is that a strip three times as long as the finished smocking will be needed in addition to the main fabric.

Design

Designing is a creative process, not a finished product. It changes as it grows. Seldom can I tell what a finished project will look like before I begin it. I start in a general direction and know the feeling I want to achieve. Most of my work is based on what feels good.

With all the theory I will present here, my "bottom line" is what feels right. This is sometimes impossible to explain to another person. My goal in this presentation is to give information that might expand your awareness and sensitivity to basic elements of designing. One idea always leads to another, and through the sharing of many ideas we will all benefit.

The creation of a design is the process of integrating several interrelated elements into a unit. The elements of line, shape, color, and space are used to produce the rhythm, proportion, balance, and emphasis within a design. The relationship of these elements gives the vitality to the total project.

Smocking designs are formed as a result of the particular placement of rows of stitches to form a motif. Usually there is a Key or Base Row, which is worked first. The secondary rows are worked in relation to the Base Row. Base Rows are generally worked with Straight stitches, while secondary rows may be Zigzag stitches. There may be several Base Rows within one motif and several motifs may be in one principal design. The repetition of a line, pattern, or color throughout the motifs will create a visual movement or rhythm throughout the design, which will hold the motifs together. There may be several rows which combine to form a balanced motif within the total design and which could be used with the rest of the design. These may be suitable for cuffs and for projects that only require a few rows of smocking.

The lines and shapes of the smocking designs are formed through the limitless combination of smocking stitches. Rows of Straight stitches and parallel rows of Zigzag stitches will create lines, while two reversed rows of Zigzag stitches create shapes such as diamonds and lattices. The size, quantity, and mass of the lines and shapes form the framework of the design. The proportions of all the elements (line, shape, color, and space) should be balanced to give a feeling of equilibrium within the design. In symmetrical designs, this is easier than in asymmetrical designs. There are numerous examples of both throughout the book.

Once the basic frame of the design has been built, shapes and lines can be emphasized with Fill-In stitches, such as Lazy Daisies, Satin stitches, Flowerettes, and French Knots. The Fill-In technique is used to attract attention to the main theme of the design, giving it more depth and artistic appeal.

The background pleats provide an element of space in the design. They give it texture and pattern. In "positive space," the pleats are held in distinct patterns which may become a focal point of the design. In some designs they are held in close vertical formations, while in others, sharp, angular patterns. At times the pleats will be allowed to puff out so that the original sharp pleat is lost. In "negative space," where there is no smocking design, backsmocking (see page 30) can be used to hold the pleats and to create a "shadow" pattern which appears in the pleats when the smocked project is pulled to its final shape. The dress in Figure 3-81 and the "Susan B" dress are excellent examples of how this technique can be used effectively.

In a one-color design, the choice of stitches must create the rhythm, proportion, emphasis, and balance of the design. The shape, lines, and space must work together. Examples are the Two Evening-Out Dresses. This approach is a challenge and will increase your awareness of how the stitches can function.

Color

No discussion of design can be complete without a thorough discussion of color and how color works. One's experience of color is the most important tool of any art. It is the interaction of color that is a key to the success of a project. One's perception of color is a subjective visual experience that can be developed through practice and observation. There are many color theories, but the best way to learn about color is to observe what happens to colors as they interact. As the threads of color are stitched into the fabric, the colors will be influenced by the background fabric and the surrounding colors.

Color is used with line, shape, and space to create the rhythm, proportion, and balance of a design. The expression of all the elements is a subjective, personal, creative process. One color may either enhance or destroy the unity of a design. Some colors may be too strong for the design and may jump out or cause the design to look spotty. On the other hand, a repeated row of bright, intense color worked with a Straight stitch can create balance and rhythm through a design. Neutral shades or subtle colors may work to create a theme which holds all the elements of the design together. The proportion of each color will change the appearance of the total design. Shapes within the design can be defined or concealed with the use of color.

When selecting colors for a design, remember that no color stands alone. Each color is affected by the adjacent colors and by the background. Though the perception of each color hue will vary from person to person, the color wheel graphically illustrates the relationships of colors. (See Figures 2-1 and 2-2.) Each circle represents the abstract idea of pure color, or hue. A well-balanced color scheme will lead to a harmonious application of some simple color principles.

A color wheel is an excellent aid in selecting colors. The hues of the color wheel are the pure colors as they appear in the light spectrum of a prism—red, orange, yellow, green, blue, indigo, and violet. The primary colors are the colors which cannot be obtained from the blend of other colors—red, yellow, and blue. Secondary colors are the colors which can be obtained from the mixture of equal proportions of two primary colors—orange (from red and yellow), green (from blue and yellow), and violet (from blue and red). Tertiary colors are a group of six variations obtained by mixing a primary color with the adjacent secondary color. These are also represented on the color diagram—yellow-green, blue-green, blue-violet, red-

2-1 A color wheel is a helpful aid to determining color schemes.

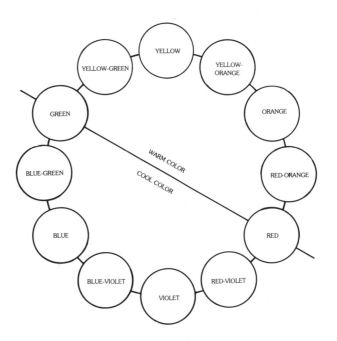

2-2 A simplified color wheel.

violet, red-orange, and yellow-orange. Complementary colors are colors that are directly opposite each other on a color wheel—yellow and violet, red and green, blue-green and red-orange, and so forth. Analogous colors are colors that are next to each other and share a common hue, such as these three—red-violet, red, and red-orange.

Each hue has a wide range of color value from light to dark. Red can range from a very light pink to a very dark red, but all are within the same hue. If several different hues are used within a design, the values of hues may be equal. However, several values of one hue may be used to increase the depth of the design.

The intensity or saturation of a color ranges from very bright to dull or muted. Look at the contrast of a bright pink next to a muted pink. Often a color seems to jump out of the design, at the expense of the other colors. The design will work better if a less intense shade is substituted. This change can save a design, making it hang together and work as a total unit.

Colors have emotional, as well as physical, properties. The mood of the total project can be set with the choice of color intensity. Intense, bright colors express gaiety, while less intense, subtle colors usually express seriousness. Delicate grays are quieter than full-strength contrasting colors which seem to vibrate with energy. Analogous colors of equal value and intensity will melt together. A discordant color, one of the original colors in a different value, will enliven and give vitality to the combination of colors. Vitality and tension within a design come from contrast—a bright

color next to a dull color, a warm against a cool, opposing colors next to each other, or a light against a dark.

Color harmony is the successful interaction between the colors within the design. The best way to learn how colors work is to observe what happens to colors in different designs. Then take groups of colors and really look at them with different fabrics and in different lights.

To achieve successful visual balance within a design, it is necessary to work out the most successful color arrangement. Before smocking complete rows, work 2 or 3 inches (5 or 8 cm) of the total design so that the colors and spacing can be adjusted. Color distribution has a direct effect on the balance and rhythm of the design.

The simplest use of color is a monochromatic scheme in which only one hue with several value changes is used. The Mother-of-the-Bride's Gown is

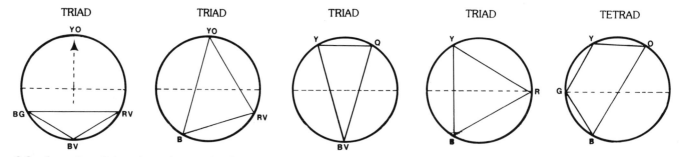

2-3 a through e Color relationships can be clearly seen when you draw lines across a color wheel.

a good example of a harmonious monochromatic scheme. If green is added to the scheme, it becomes a complementary scheme. In the Flower-Girl Gown, the complementary green gives definition, the two values of red create contrast, and the neutral brown creates the basic theme. The deep rose is a discordant color because it is a different tonal value from the green and light pink. The contrast enhances the design.

In both designs the deep rose has the highest intensity which dominates the colors of less intensity.

The designs in the Lady's Pinafore and Little Girl's Dress (see Two Old-Fashioned Looks) illustrate the harmonious effect of an analogous color scheme that is enlivened with a discordant color. All the colors share a common hue of blue. Analogous colors tend to be soft and melt together, but would be flat and uninteresting if there were no contrast. The light violet is the discordant color introduced to give the design tension and vitality. The dark violet provides the rhythm, while the light violet helps emphasize the theme. The green and blue create the shape and basic framework.

In the pinafore a complementary shade of yellow-orange is introduced to the total project in the print of the blouse. The smocking design would stand alone as a pleasing harmonious design, but, when the blouse is added, the project is enhanced by the introduction of the complementary color.

The interrelationship of colors in a color scheme can be represented schematically. If you draw lines across a color wheel to connect the colors in your scheme, you will arrive at different shapes. (See Fig-

ures 2-3a through e.) An equilateral triangle means you have a triad, which is three colors of equal value. Triads have the highest intensity. These colors intensify each other and make the contrast seem even greater. They relate a feeling of energy, gaiety, and life. Red, yellow, and blue together are a triad. A tetrad is four colors in the circle, of equal value, which form a parallelogram.

See the Three Sundresses in Part 3. In the blue sundress the blue comes from the background fabric and white is added to accent the design. The orange sundress illustrates a second type of triad which forms an isosceles triangle. The sundress with the black insert illustrates the dramatic effect of color against a black background where images often seem to float. The colors in this project do not form a true equilateral triangle, but are nevertheless harmonious and dramatic.

Observe the relationship of the colors in the Hooded Caftan. This is an example of a tetrad. A tetrad has the same high intensity as a triad only with four colors instead of three. Getting back to our example, blue is the dominant color and is used to create the framework and theme of the design. The complementary orange is used in only four rows, but gives the rhythm and unites the total design. The yellow gives emphasis to a specific focal point, while green is used to build the central theme. Without any one of these elements, the design would lose its impact and intensity. These four colors are an excellent example of a tetrad. In this design the colors and shapes create a balanced asymmetrical design.

The Design Graph:
An Aid to Design and Color

Now that you are familiar with many of the concepts that must be integrated into a completed project, you will find the graphs accompanying each project to be an invaluable aid. Each graph illustrates the placement of the rows of stitches, their relationship to the gathering threads and to the adjacent rows of stitches. The labeling (see Reading Design Graphs in Part 1) tells you what stitch and color to use on each row. If you study each graph, you will begin to see combinations of stitches forming shapes that work together to form motifs within the larger design. These can be used in combinations of other stitches to build a totally new design. In this way you begin to become your own designer. As you study the graphs, see if you can spot the elements (line, shape, and space) that produce the rhythm, proportion, balance, and emphasis within the design.

Working a design on a graph before beginning to smock will save a lot of time and will help you determine how many rows will be needed to pleat. The Base Rows are the first rows of the design to be worked and all other rows are added to or are built around the Base Row as the design begins to take shape.

A second method for developing a design is to graph a background with a Zigzag stitch and begin to experiment with different Fill-In stitches. Often the Fill-In stitches create the rhythm and emphasize a space. Graphs can be exciting to work with and help you to experiment with many possibilities. Special graph paper is available where smocking supplies are sold.

Construction

By following a few basic rules smocking can be incorporated into standard commercial patterns. The methods of construction for decorative and functional smocking vary, as will be illustrated here. For either, once adjustments have been made to the pattern, the finishing construction will be the same as for conventional sewing. You may wish to refer to a basic sewing book for finishing methods.

Decorative Smocking

For decorative smocking a smocked strip or insert is incorporated into the garment as a decorative detail.

The smocking is not used to control the fullness of the fabric.

1 Select a basic shirtwaist pattern with no pleats or gathers.
2 Draw in where the insert will be placed on the pattern. (See Figure 2-4 a and b for different possibilities.) These lines will be the new stitching lines. Draw the ⅝-inch (1.5 cm) seam allowances for the garment. Cut out the areas where the insert will be placed along seam allowance lines. (See Figure 2-5.)

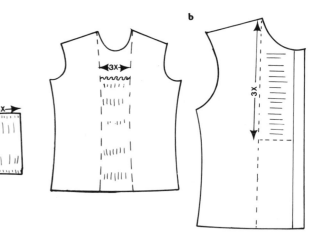

2-4 a and b a) For half designs measure across the longest point where the insert will have to spread. Multiply by six for the width of fabric that will have to be pleated; b) For full designs measure across the area where the insert will have to spread. Multiply by three for the full width that must be pleated.

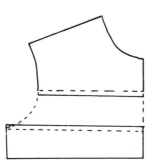

2-5 Cut out the area where the insert will be placed.

3 Decide whether the pleats will run horizontally or vertically. Measure across the longest point where the insert will have to spread. Multiply this measurement by either three or six: if the pattern is a full front, multiply by three; if it is half the front, by six. (Refer to Figure 2-4 for examples.) This will give you the length of fabric needed for the insert. Measure across the area on the pattern from stitchline to stitchline. Add seam allowances and this will be the width. Note: a three-to-one ratio is only a rule of thumb (3 inches of fabric for 1 inch of finished smocking). The ratio will change according to fabric. Lightweight fabrics can go up to six-to-one, while heavier fabrics can be two-and-one-half-to-one. Two or more strips of

fabric can be sewn together to make a longer insert, if needed. When deciding how much fabric you will need, remember that the more pleats you have in an area, the more stitches there will be in that area. This means you will have a more concentrated design.

4 Pleat your fabric according to the instructions in Part 1.

5 Smock, following the graphed design.

6 Block to the finished width, following instructions in Part 1.

7 Choose one of the following three methods for stitching the insert to the fabric pieces. Any one of the methods will help to prevent puckering.

PIPING
The seam between the smocked insert and garment can be reinforced with piping. This will make a neat straight seam and prevent puckering.

a Use a commercial piping or make your own. To do so, cover two or three strands of prewashed cotton string with the same fabric as the garment or with a contrasting fabric. (Use one strand for infants' small size garments.) Cut piping the same length as the seams.

b Baste the piping along the top and bottom row of smocking.

2-6 Stitch the piping to the insert.

c Using the zipper foot on your sewing machine, stitch the piping to the insert. (See Figure 2-6.)

d With right sides together, place garment fabric over insert and piping. Using the ridge of the piping as a guide, stitch along the seamline. (See Figure 2-7.)

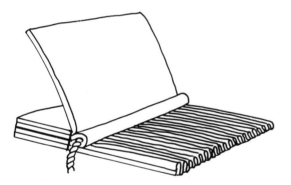

2-7 Place the fabric over the piping and stitch along the gathered edge.

e Trim seams as illustrated. (See Figure 2-8.) Fold back and press. Stay-stitch along armhole curve and trim.

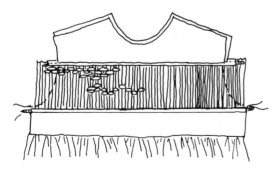

2-8 Stay-stitch along armhole curve and trim.

CONTRASTING BANDS

Contrasting bands not only help reinforce the joining seam, but also visually frame the smocking.

a Baste the smocked piece onto the right side of fabric. Make sure the smocking is straight.
b Stitch around the outside rows of smocking. Trim.
c Cut contrasting bands of fabric to cover edges of smocked piece. Line with interfacing. Press under seam allowances.
d Place bands along top and bottom of insert and baste into place. Topstitch with double rows of stitching. (See Figure 2-9.)

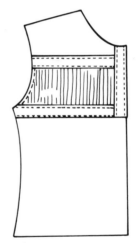

2-9 Stitch bands around the edge and topstitch.

e Reinforce the seam by making a double row of stitching, by running a machine zigzag stitch, or by covering the seam with seam binding. (See Figure 2-10.)

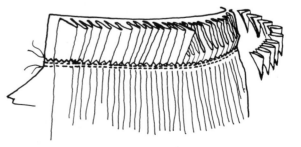

2-10 Reinforce the seams and trim.

GARMENT SEWN DIRECTLY TO INSERT

There may be times when you may not want to use either of the first two methods. If the seams are properly reinforced, there should be no reason why you can't sew the garment directly to the insert.

   a After the smocked insert has been blocked, run a basting thread along the top row of smocking to be used as a stitching guide.
   b Place insert across right side of fabric. Baste in place. (See Figure 2-11.)
   c Stitch along the basted stitching guide. Press and trim.
   d Follow steps for Contrasting Bands.
8 Finish the construction of the garment as you would have without the insert.

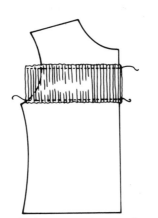

2-11 Baste the smocked insert in place on the garment.

Functional Smocking

Functional smocking can be applied to a garment in any area where full fabric is held close to the body or gathered into a seam. The following examples will help illustrate the main principles, which can be applied to other projects.

BASIC YOKE

1 Start with a basic shirtwaist pattern. Draw a line where the bottom of the yoke should be. Cut out, adding seam allowances. (See Figure 2-12.)

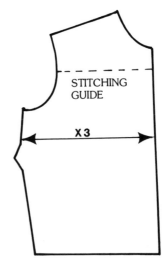

2-12 A basic fitted bodice pattern. Measure across the widest point of the pattern and multiply by three.

2 Measure across the widest part of the pattern. Multiply by three and add seam allowances to get the amount of fabric you will need. Cut out this amount of fabric. (See Figure 2-13.) Cut out a square, disregarding the dart and armholes.

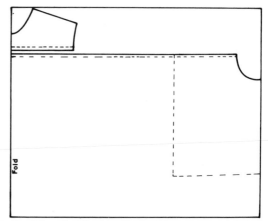

2-13 Cut fabric for the smocked pieces.

3 Pleat according to instructions in Part 1.
4 Smock according to your graph.
5 Pull out gathering threads. Block to the same width as the widest part of the pattern, following instructions in Part 1.

6 Place a tissue pattern over the blocked smocking. Stay-stitch along the edge of the curve. (See Figure 2-14.)

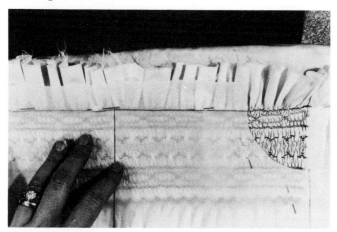

2-14 Place tissue pattern over blocked smocking, and stay-stitch along armhole curve.

7 Cut about ⅝ inch (1.5 cm) outside the stay-stitching. The smocking will not pull out. (See Figure 2-15.)

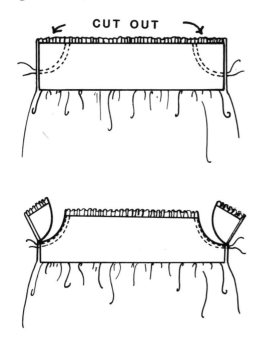

2-15 Cut ⅝ inch (1.6cm) outside of stay-stitching.

8 With wrong sides together, fold bias strips in half lengthwise and press lightly. Place 1/16-inch cord in the fold of the bias strip and baste firmly. Using a zipper or cording foot, stitch close to cord. (See Figure 2-16.) With right sides together, pin center

2-16 Place cord in bias strip and stitch close to cord.

of piping to center of smocked front piece. Baste piping across, next to the top row of smocking. Stitch close to the piping, using a zipper or cording foot. (See Figure 2-17.)

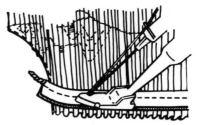

2-17 Stitch piping to the smocked front piece.

9 With right sides together, baste the yoke to the smocked front. (See Figure 2-18.) Next, baste the right side of yoke lining to the wrong side of

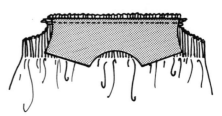

2-18 Baste the yoke to the smocked front, with right sides together.

smocked front. (See Figure 2-19.) Stitch through all three pieces, using the ridge of the piping to guide the zipper foot.

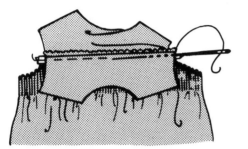

2-19 Baste the right side of yoke lining to the wrong side of smocked front.

10 Press the yokes up. (See Figure 2-20.)

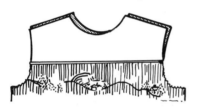

2-20 Press the yokes up.

11 Prepare piping as above for the back piece and stitch the piping across the back as you did for the front. (See Figure 2-21.) Stay-stitch along the edge of the unsmocked pleats, tapering to a point at the center. Cut an opening between the stitching (instructions will usually tell you to leave

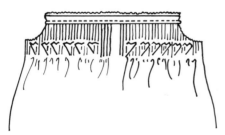

2-21 Stitch piping across the back piece.

two or three pleats unstitched for this purpose), being careful not to cut the stay-stitching at the point. (See Figure 2-22.)

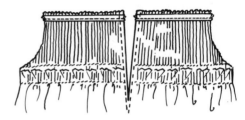

2-22 Cut an opening between the stitching on the smocked piece.

12 Pin the wrong side of the back opening to the right side of the placket bias strip so that the stay-stiching is ¼ inch (6 mm) from the edge of the strip. Baste and stitch. (See Figure 2-23.) Press the

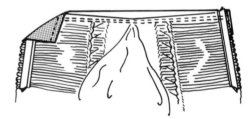

2-23 Baste and stitch the placket bias strip to the wrong side of the back opening.

seam and strip up. Press the raw edge down ¼ inch (6 mm). Fold the strip so that the fold edge lines up with the line of stitching. Baste and stitch. (See Figure 2-24.) Turn the left side of placket to

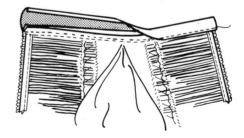

2-24 Fold the placket bias strip over; baste and stitch.

the inside of dress and baste across the top. Slip-stitch the folded edge to the dress. (See Figure 2-25.)

2-25 Turn the left side of the placket to the inside and baste across the top; then slip-stitch.

13 Fold the back yoke in half with right sides together. Place folded back yoke around the back opening and baste. (See Figure 2-26.) Stitch through all

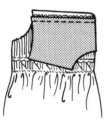

2-26 Place the folded back yoke around the back opening and baste.

thicknesses, using the ridge of the piping to guide the zipper foot. Trim. Turn the yoke right side out so that the fold is even with the back opening and press up. (See Figure 2-27.)

2-27 Turn the yoke right side out and press up.

14 Follow the same procedure for the right side, except the right side of placket is not turned to the inside. (See Figure 2-28.)

2-28 Prepare the right side of the placket.

15 With right sides together, stitch front and back yoke at shoulder seams. Turn and press open. (See Figure 2-29.)

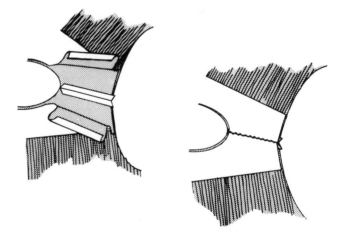

2-29 Stitch front and back yokes at shoulder seams; then turn and press open.

2-30 Slip-stitch yoke linings together at shoulder seams.

16 Press under shoulder seam allowance of front and back yoke linings. Trim ¼ inch.

17 Slip-stitch yoke linings together at shoulder seams. (See Figure 2-30.)

18 Finish construction of dress according to pattern instructions.

SMOCKING FROM THE SHOULDER SEAM

1 Start with a basic shirtwaist pattern. Measure across the widest part of the pattern and multiply by three to get the amount of fabric you will need. Add ⅝ inch (1.5 cm) for seam allowances.

2 Cut a square the new width and the length you need for the shirt or dress you are making. The length will not change.

3 Pleat, following directions in Part 1.

4 Smock, following your Design Graph.

5 Block the square of smocking as wide as the widest point on the pattern, following directions in Part 1.

6 Using the original basic shirtwaist pattern, cut a front lining. Stitch in all darts.

7 With wrong sides together, pin the lining to the blocked smocking. Stay-stitch around the seamlines. Cut out arm and neck curves. (See Figure 2-31 a and b.)

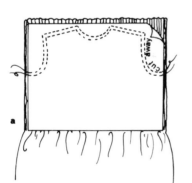

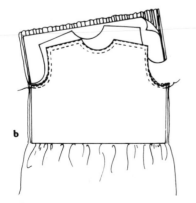

2-31 a and b a) Pin the tissue pattern to the blocked smocking and stay-stitch around the seamlines. b) Cut out arm and neck curves.

8 For the back opening, mark a 4-inch-long (10 cm) center back line on the straight grain of the fabric. Stay-stitch ¼ inch (6 mm) from the center back, tapering to a point. Take one or two stitches across the end and stitch up the other side. Slash the opening between stitching, being careful not to cut the stay-stitching at the point. (See Figure 2-32.)

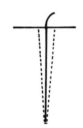

2-32 Cut an opening between the stitching, being careful not to cut the stay-stitching.

9 With right sides together, pin the opening to the bias placket strip, so that the stay-stitch is ¼ inch (6 mm) from the edge of the strip. Baste and stitch. (See Figure 2-33.)

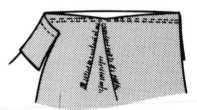

2-33 Baste and stitch the opening to the bias placket strip.

10 Press the strip over the raw edge of seam allowance. Turn work over and press ¼ inch (6 mm) of the free edge of the strip under. (See Figure 2-34 a and b.)

11 Stitch two rows of running stitch or machine basting along the top of the skirt and pull threads to gather.

12 With right sides together, pin skirt to back bodice,

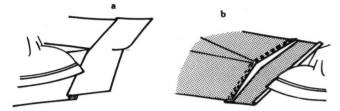

2-34 a and b a) Press the strip over the seam allowance. b) Turn the strip over; press ¼ inch of the free edge of strip under.

placing the edge of the placket on the foldline of right back bodice facing, and ⅝ inch (1.5 cm) from foldline of left back bodice facing. Distribute the fullness evenly between dot markings on the back bodice. Baste and stitch. Trim seams. (See Figure 2-35.)

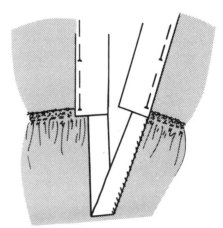

2-36 Fold back facings over the skirt placket.

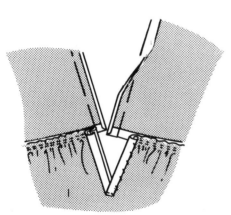

2-35 Pin skirt to back bodice, distributing the fullness; baste and stitch.

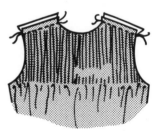

2-37 Stitch front and back together at shoulder seams.

13 Fold back facings over the skirt placket. (See Figure 2-36.) Pin into place, but do not stitch at this time.

14 With right sides together, stitch front and back together at shoulder seams. Trim. (See Figure 2-37.) Press seams toward back.

15 With right sides together, pin and baste sleeves to dress, matching dot markings and shoulder seams, pulling up machine stitchings to fit. Stitch. (See Figure 2-38.)

16 Finish the dress according to pattern instructions.

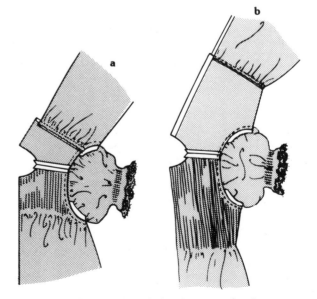

2-38 a and b Baste and stitch the sleeves to the dress.

ROUND YOKES

1 Start with a basic raglan sleeve pattern. (See Figure 2-39.)

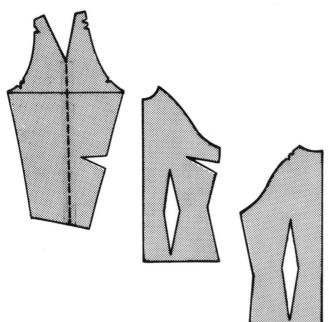

2-39 A basic raglan sleeve pattern.

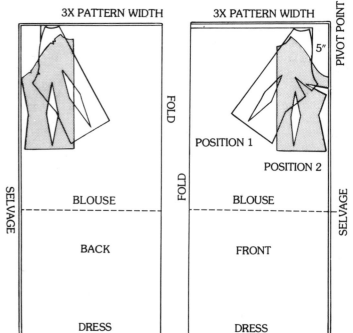

2-40 To draw the new armhole curve place the pattern so that the neck curve is on the top line. Then pivot the pattern so that it is straight up and down.

2 Measure the width of the pattern 5 inches below the neckline curve. For the width of the fabric you will need to multiply the width of the pattern by three. Place the armhole curve of the pattern so that the upper portion is parallel to the straight edge of the fabric. The length from the hemline to the bottom of the armhole must be the same on the front and the back. The top edges, or neck edge, is drawn straight from the top of the armhole curves. The front will be 1 inch (2.5 cm) lower than the back. (See Figure 2-40.)

3 For the sleeves, place each armhole curve so that the lower point of each is level with the other. Draw a line between the tops of each curve. (See Figure 2-41.) The lower edge can be square. Work a ⅛-inch rolled hem along the bottom edge of sleeves.

4 Following directions in Part 1, pleat around yoke and sleeve cuff.

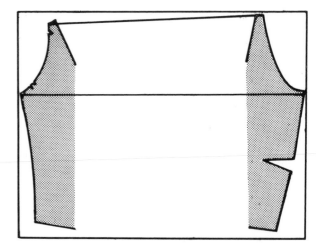

2-41 Draw a line between the top of each armhole curve.

5 Being careful not to catch the gathering threads, stitch sleeves to armhole edge of fronts and backs, making French seams. Match all rows. (See Figure 2-42.)

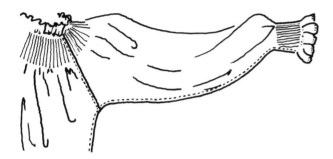

2-42 Stitch sleeves to armhole edge of fronts and backs.

6 Pull gathering threads so that the fabric forms a tube shape. Do not panic! Your design will form a curve if the last five or six rows are Zigzag stitches, you only picked up one-third of the pleats, your tension was not too tight, and you allowed enough fabric.

7 Stitch underarm seams of garment and sleeves, making French seams. Smock around yoke and sleeves, continuing to smock over the seams.

8 After the smocking has been completed, pull out the gathering threads and block into a curve. Lay garment flat on an ironing board. Spread yoke into a circle. Block.

9 If you have binding around the neck, construct the binding and placket. After the bias binding has been stitched around the neck seamline, trim evenly 3/16 inch (7 mm) from the seamline, then roll the bias binding tightly over the edge and slip-stitch on the inside.

10 Pull out gathering threads and steam into shape.

11 Finish the dress according to pattern instructions. Extra care should be used in blocking to make sure the yoke will lie flat and will not ride up around the neck.

SMOCKING ON A SLEEVE OR CUFF

1 Choose a basic cap or tailored sleeve pattern. Measure around the area of the arm to be covered. (See Figure 2-43.) Ratio of fabric for the

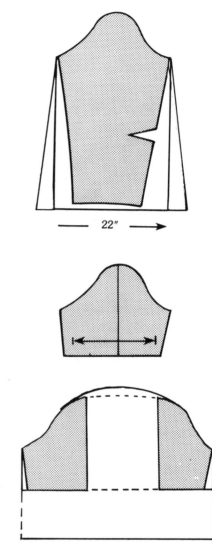

2-43 Basic cap sleeve pattern.

fullness of the sleeve or cuff to this measurement may be three-to-one, or four-to-one, or five-to-one, depending on the weight of the fabric.

2 Flare the sleeve to the desired fullness. Allow at least 22 inches around the wrist. Add 1 inch at the bottom of the ruffle.

3 To make a modified "leg-of-mutton" sleeve, allow fullness for smocking and extend the bottom of the sleeve 6 to 8 inches (15 to 20 cm) for the ruffle.

NECK PLACKET

1 Complete smocking and pull out gathering threads.

2 Make five loops from a 6-inch (15-cm) bias strip, long enough to go around any buttons you choose to use. (See Figure 2-44.)

2-44 Stitching a loop.

3 Stay-stitch along the edge of the unsmocked pleats, forming a point at center back. Slash between stitching. (See Figure 2-45.)

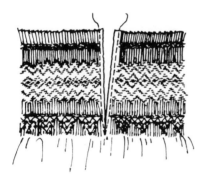

2-45 Slash an opening between the stitching.

4 Cut a strip of fabric twice the length of the back opening. Baste the strip to the inside of the slashed opening. Place the edge of the slashed opening ¼ inch (6 mm) from the edge of the strip and stitch. (See Figure 2-46.)

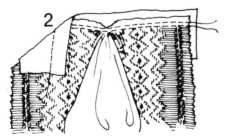

2-46 Stitch the slashed opening and the strip.

5 Baste loops into place. (See Figure 2-47.)

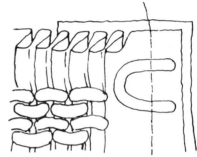

2-47 Baste the loops into place.

6 Turn under ¼ inch of strip, fold, and topstitch. (See Figure 2-48.)

7 Turn left side to the inside and baste.

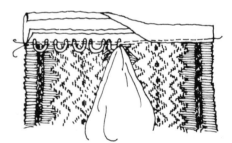

2-48 Turn under strip; fold, and topstitch.

NECK BINDING

1 Cut a bias strip 16 inches (40 cm) long. (If you need a longer neckline, adjust accordingly.)

2 Stitch a running stitch around the neck. Gather to desired size.

3 Pin edge of binding to neck edge. Stitch binding so it is even with the first row of smocking. Stitch and trim evenly. (See Figure 2-49.) Turn under.

2-49 Pin the edge of binding to neck edge; stitch and trim.

4 Turn binding tightly over edge. Slip-stitch on inside. (See Figure 2-50.)

2-50 Turn binding over edge and slipstitch on inside.

A Summary of Differences

The following is a capsulization of the differences between decorative and functional smocking:

DECORATIVE SMOCKING
1 The smocking is added for ornamentation.

2 The smocking does not affect the shape of the garment.

FUNCTIONAL SMOCKING
1 Smocking controls and shapes the fullness of the fabric to fit the body.

2 The smocking fundamentally affects the shape of the garment.

3 Extra fabric is needed for the insert only.

4 The insert may be a lightweight fabric; the garment can be a heavier fabric—as heavy as corduroy or suede.

5 Smocking is stabilized between two pieces of fabric.

6 After the insert is sewn into place, the construction of the garment is the same as the original pattern.

3 Extra fabric must be allowed for fullness.

4 The weight and drape of the fabric must be considered when choosing the fabric.

5 The elasticity of the smocking is utilized to hold and shape the garment to the body.

6 Some special construction techniques may have to be used.

A Sample Project: Smocked Pillow

You now have many facts and techniques swimming around in your head. But where do you start so that you are not in deep water before you are sure you know how to swim? Any one of the four pillows shown here (see Figure 2-51) would make a good beginner project. They cover all the basic stitches, but Pillows 2 and 3 introduce Zigzags and Crossovers.

MATERIALS
1 piece fabric, 6 by 22 inches (15 by 56 cm), for smocked center
2 pieces fabric, each 12 by 15 inches (30 by 38 cm), for front and back
eyelet and contrasting fabric bands to go around pillow
1 skein embroidery floss in each of the colors specified on Design Graph
stuffing

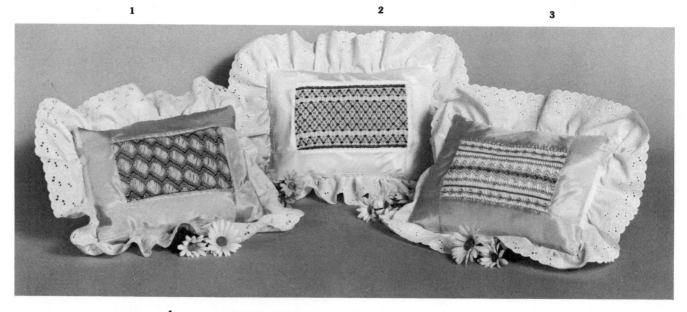

2-51 Choose one of these four smocked insert pillows as your first sample project.

2-52 Method 1 of making the sample pillow.

DIRECTIONS

Method 1

1. Cut sampler, pleat, and smock.
2. Block and baste to a backing. Stitch ribbons along the edges. (See Figure 2-52.) Stitch eyelet around outer edge.
3. Stitch backing and stuff.

Method 2

1. Cut sampler, pleat, and smock.
2. Draw a window in the fabric backing.
3. Stitch around the edges.
4. Cut open. Clip corners.
5. Press edges under. Baste sampler into place.
6. Sew each seam separately, following the number sequence as illustrated. (See Figure 2-53.)

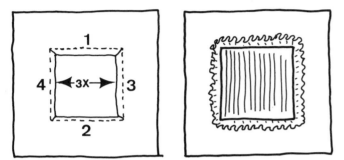

7 Stitch eyelet around the edges.
8 Stitch backing and stuff.

2-53 Method 2 of making the sample pillow.

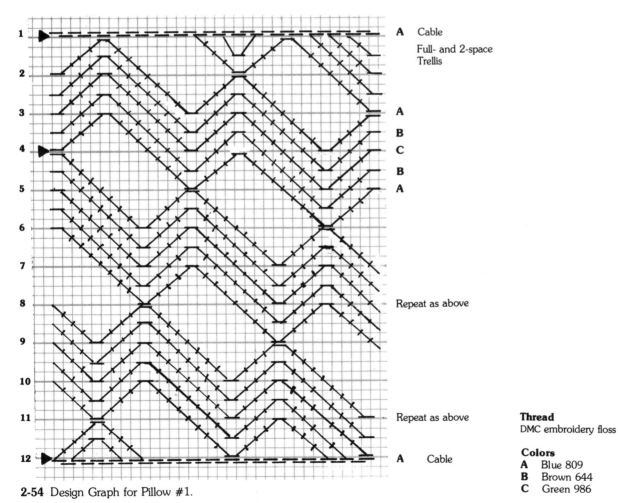

A Cable

Full- and 2-space
Trellis

A

B

C

B

A

Repeat as above

Repeat as above

A Cable

2-54 Design Graph for Pillow #1.

Thread
DMC embroidery floss

Colors
A Blue 809
B Brown 644
C Green 986

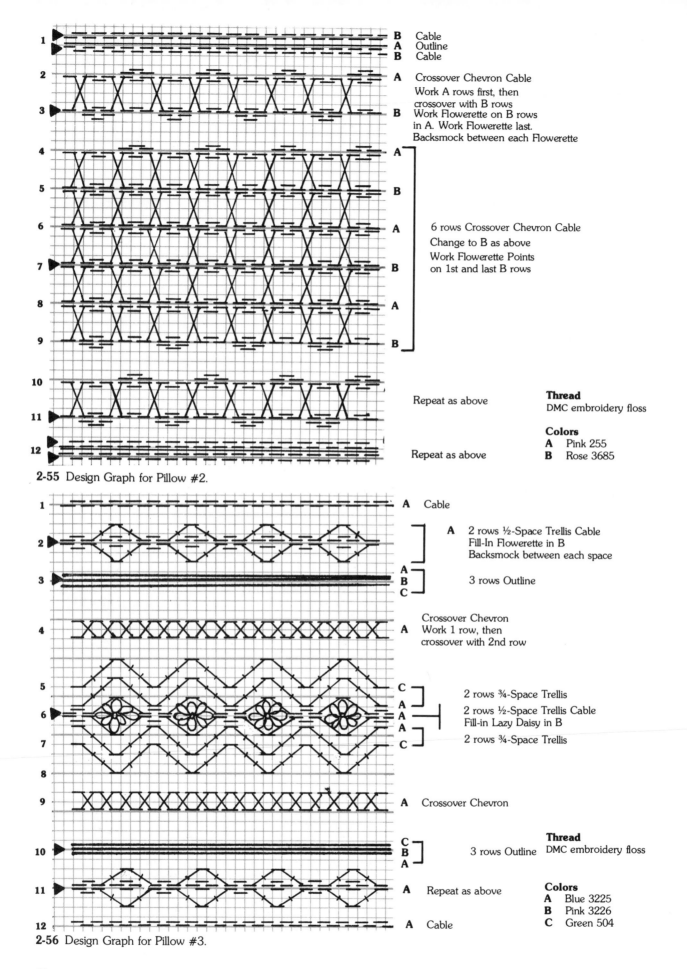

1   **B**   Cable
A   Outline
B   Cable

2   **A**   Crossover Chevron Cable
Work A rows first, then
crossover with B rows
3   **B**   Work Flowerette on B rows
in A. Work Flowerette last.
Backsmock between each Flowerette

4   **A**

5   **B**

6   **A**   6 rows Crossover Chevron Cable
Change to B as above
Work Flowerette Points
7   **B**   on 1st and last B rows

8   **A**

9   **B**

10

11   Repeat as above

Thread
DMC embroidery floss

Colors
A   Pink 255
12   Repeat as above   **B**   Rose 3685

2-55 Design Graph for Pillow #2.

1   **A**   Cable

2   **A**   2 rows ½-Space Trellis Cable
Fill-In Flowerette in B
Backsmock between each space

3   **A**
B   3 rows Outline
C

4   **A**   Crossover Chevron
Work 1 row, then
crossover with 2nd row

5   **C**   2 rows ¾-Space Trellis
6   **A**
     A   2 rows ½-Space Trellis Cable
     A   Fill-in Lazy Daisy in B
7   **C**   2 rows ¾-Space Trellis

8

9   **A**   Crossover Chevron

Thread
10   **C**
     B   3 rows Outline   DMC embroidery floss
     A

Colors
11   **A**   Repeat as above   **A**   Blue 3225
                                        B   Pink 3226
12   **A**   Cable   **C**   Green 504

2-56 Design Graph for Pillow #3.

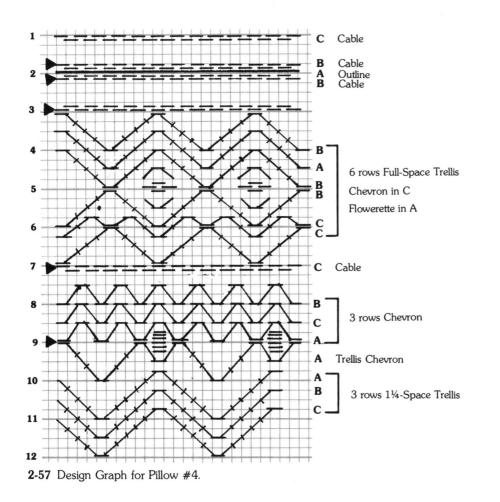

Row	Label	Stitch/Description
1	C	Cable
2	B	Cable
	A	Outline
	B	Cable
3	C	Cable
4–6	B A B B C C	6 rows Full-Space Trellis Chevron in C Flowerette in A
7	C	Cable
8–9	B C A	3 rows Chevron
9	A	Trellis Chevron
10–11	A B C	3 rows 1¼-Space Trellis

2-57 Design Graph for Pillow #4.

Thread
DMC embroidery floss

Colors
A Red 666
B Yellow 726
C Green 911
D Gold 741
E Green 890

A Sample Project: Smocked Christmas Ball

A Christmas ornament is another good beginning project. You can stuff a smocked piece of fabric with a 3- or 4-inch Styrofoam ball. Then decorate it with extra pearls or beads and trim it with lace and ribbons. Another possibility is to stuff a wiffle ball into the center and fill it with potpourri, or scoop out a Styrofoam ball and place a music box inside. The ends of the ball can be finished with Spider Webs or a piece of holly. Use your imagination and come up with even more variations on this idea. (See Figure 2-58.)

MATERIALS

    1 piece of fabric, 7 by 27 inches (18 by 69 cm), to be pleated and smocked

    1½ yds (1.5 m) ribbon, white

    1 skein embroidery floss each in red and white Styrofoam ball

2-58 A smocked Christmas ball makes a special decoration and is a good starter project for beginners.

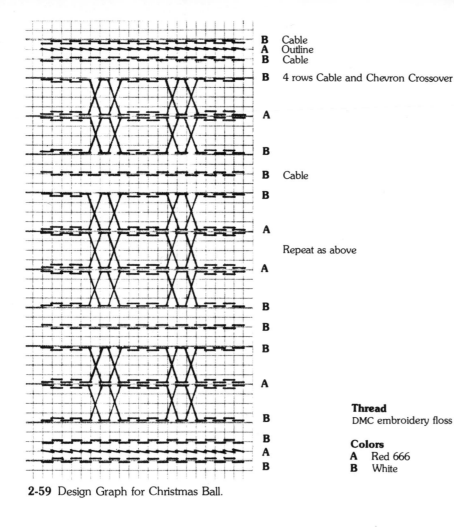

B Cable
A Outline
B Cable

B 4 rows Cable and Chevron Crossover

A

B

B Cable

B

A

Repeat as above

A

B

B

B

A

Thread
DMC embroidery floss

B

Colors
A Red 666
B White

A

B

B

A

B

2-59 Design Graph for Christmas Ball.

DIRECTIONS

1 Pleat and smock the fabric, following the Design Graph. (See Figure 2-59.)

2 Pull out all gathering threads, except the first and last two rows.

3 Slip-stitch pleats so that the design matches and smocking forms a tube, as illustrated. (See Figure 2-60.) Bring the two ends of the sampler together.

4 Push a Styrofoam ball into the smocked tube.

5 Pull gathering threads at the top and bottom so that the smocking fits around the ball. Trim edges evenly, so that they do not overlap. Using sewing thread the same color as the fabric, run a basting thread along entire edge. Pull tight, and stitch back and forth across the opening, until the raw edges lie flat. (See Figure 2-61.)

6 Work a Whipped Spider Web over the raw edges at one end. (See Figures 2-62 and 2-63.) Make a bow for the other end. (See Figure 2-64.) Secure in the middle with a pin.

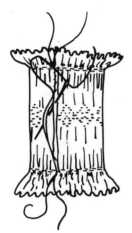

2-63 A Whipped Spider Web

2-60 Bring the ends of the smocked piece together so that it forms a tube and slip-stitch together.

2-64 Make a bow for the other end.

2-61 Stitch back and forth until the raw edges lie flat.

2-62 Work a Whipped Spider Web over the raw edges.

PART THREE

Smocking Projects Step by Step

Smocking has been a part of the world of fashion for many centuries. With each resurgence, this beautiful art is revived with a new spirit of creativity. From the old English smock to a dainty party dress, smocking continues to turn homemade garments into handcrafted heirlooms.

The following projects are examples of some of the ways smocking can be adapted for every member of the family. I hope these projects will inspire you to create your own heirlooms for your family and loved ones.

Two Sisters' Nightgowns

Smocking adds a feminine touch to two lovely nightgowns. (See Figure 3-1 and color section.) The big sister's gown (Nightgown #1, left) is a dusty rose crepe with a lace insertion along the bottom hem. The little sister's gown (Nightgown #2, right) is a yellow silklike synthetic with a very simple band of smocking around the yoke and sleeves. Both gowns were designed and stitched by Nellie Durand.

3-1 Little sister's yellow silky synthetic nightgown has a smocked circular yoke. Big sister's dusty rose gown has a smocked front bodice and ties at the shoulder. Both gowns were designed and stitched by Nellie Durand.

Nightgown #1

MATERIALS
Rainbow Hill Lady's Blouse Pattern #4-1278 (see Sources in back of book) or any commercial raglan sleeve pattern
3⅛ yds (2.8 m) polyester crepe fabric, rose
1 spool buttonhole silk twist, ecru
2½ yds (2.3 m) lace, ½ inch (1.3 cm)
3½ yds (3.3 m) bias binding
sewing thread to match fabric

DIRECTIONS
1　Review Construction on page 41.
2　Cut out front and back bodices, allowing extra fabric for length. Some of the fullness can be omitted, if you wish.
3　Pleat fourteen rows and smock the design. (See Figures 3-2 and 3-3.) Pull out gathering threads.
4　Stitch side seams.
5　Bind armholes with bias binding.

6 Make a binding over top of smocking 8 inches (20.3 cm) long.

7 Make four shoestring straps, attach them to gown, and tie at shoulders.

8 Stitch the lace insertion around the bottom of the gown.

9 Hem.

3-2 Detail of Nightgown #1 design.

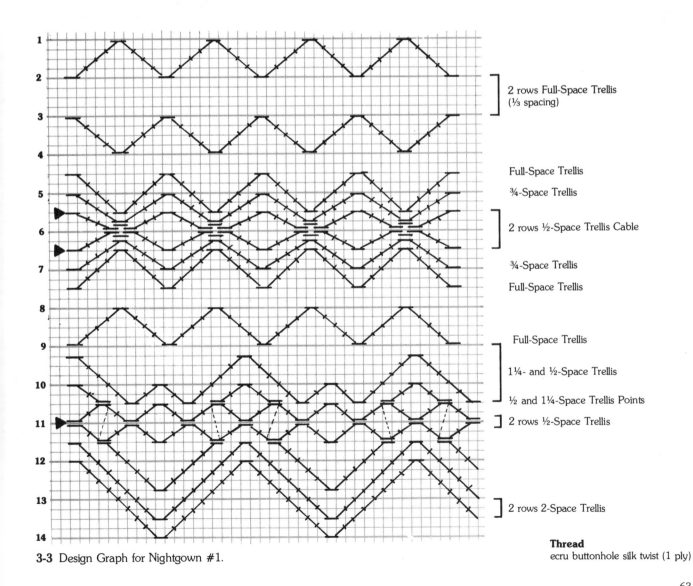

3-3 Design Graph for Nightgown #1.

2 rows Full-Space Trellis (⅓ spacing)

Full-Space Trellis

¾-Space Trellis

2 rows ½-Space Trellis Cable

¾-Space Trellis

Full-Space Trellis

Full-Space Trellis

1¼- and ½-Space Trellis

½ and 1¼-Space Trellis Points

2 rows ½-Space Trellis

2 rows 2-Space Trellis

Thread
ecru buttonhole silk twist (1 ply)

Nightgown #2

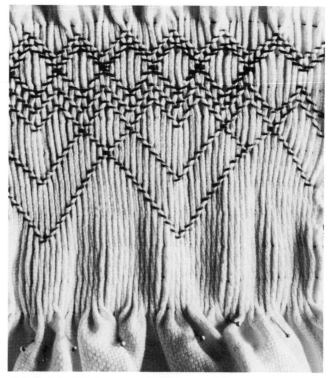

3-4 Detail of Nightgown #2 design.

MATERIALS

Rainbow Hill Lady's Blouse Pattern #4-1279 (see Sources in back of book) or any commercial raglan sleeve pattern

1 spool buttonhole silk twist, each in yellow and white

4 yds (3.6 m) synthetic silk fabric, yellow

8 yds (7.2 m) lace edging, ½ inch (1.3 cm) wide sewing thread to match fabric

DIRECTIONS

1 Review Construction on page 41.

2 Cut out pattern pieces to appropriate sizes.

3 Make rolled hems along neck ruffle and sleeves. Stitch lace to all edges. (The ruffle is formed from the upper edge of the gown.)

4 Pleat nine rows around yoke and four rows around sleeves. The neck ruffle should be ½ inch (1.3 cm) wide. (The top row should be ½ inch (1.3 cm) from the edge of the fabric. This forms the ruffle.)

5 Stitch sleeves to the armhole edges of front and back, matching all rows. Stitch the underarm seams of garment and sleeves.

6 Smock the design, starting on the first pleated row. (See Figures 3-4 and 3-5.) Backsmock around the neck with two rows of Cables.

7 Pull out gathering threads and block into a curved shape.

8 Hem and stitch lace around bottom.

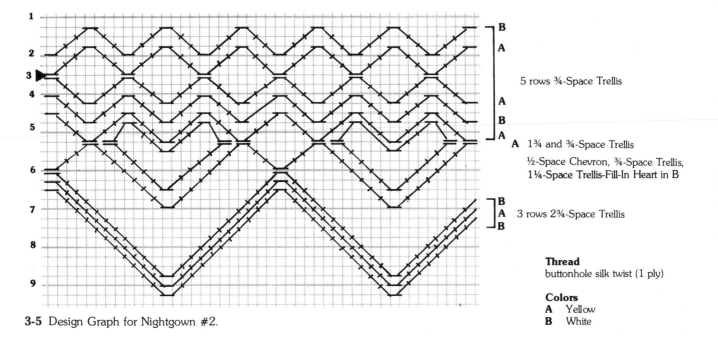

5 rows ¾-Space Trellis

A 1¾ and ¾-Space Trellis

½-Space Chevron, ¾-Space Trellis, 1¼-Space Trellis-Fill-In Heart in B

3 rows 2¾-Space Trellis

Thread
buttonhole silk twist (1 ply)

Colors
A   Yellow
B   White

3-5 Design Graph for Nightgown #2.

C-1 This Curved-Yoke Rain Jacket (see page 111) is an attractive, innovative way to utilize smocking.

C-2 Two Old-Fashioned Looks such as these are tremendous fun to create for special occasions. See page 85 for instructions.

C-3 Brother and Sister Jackets can be spruced up with the addition of some attractive smocking. Instructions are on page 101.

C-4 Both the Chevron Shirt and Dress are taught on page 105.

C-1

C-2

C-3

C-4

C-5

C-6

C-7

C-5 Three Evening-Out Dresses will make lovely additions to any wardrobe. See page 89.

C-6 This lovely Two-Toned Sundress incorporates smocking in a simple way. Instructions are on page 83.

C-7 Instructions for the China-Silk Peasant Blouse can be found on page 76. The blouse was smocked entirely in variations of Herringbone stitch.

C-8

C-9

C-8 Instructions for Two Sisters' Nightgowns are on page 62.

C-9 This Circular-Yoked Peasant Blouse (see page 67) was smocked in an attractive plaidlike design.

C-10 These Flower-Girl and Mother-of-the-Bride Gowns add a special touch to a wedding party. See instructions on page 118.

C-11 Instructions for Two Gingham Blouses can be found on page 80. It is easy to pleat gingham fabrics because the printed pattern can be followed as a guide.

C-10

C-11

C-12

C-13

C-15

C-14

C-12 Two Elegant Dresses such as these (see page 114) are sure to become wardrobe treasures.

C-13 The Three Sundresses (see page 70) shown here illustrate some of the many ways in which smocking can be incorporated in a dress.

C-14 As can be seen by these attractive Father and Son Cherokee Shirts (see page 95), smocking is not just for women and little girls.

C-15 The Hooded Caftan is a dramatic way to utilize smocking. See page 125 for instructions.

C-16 The Little Girl's "Rainbow Hill" Dress features the lovely freeform design for which it was named. See instructions on page 78.

C-16

Baby's Christening Gown

This elegant christening gown was designed for sizes six months to one year. It will be a classic heirloom. (See Figure 3-6.) The design across the front yoke was stitched in dainty Flowerettes in soft pastel colors and then backsmocked in white. There are two rows of smocking along the top of the big ruffle and the scalloped edge is trimmed in French lace. The gown should be made out of a soft batiste and the embroidery floss colors should be very soft pink, blue, and green. The gown was designed and stitched by Mary Leslie Sheeley.

MATERIALS

Rainbow Hill Pattern #17-9080 (see Sources in back of book) or basic yoked pattern

3 yds (2.7 m) polyester cotton batiste fabric (enough for gown and lining for yoke), soft white

1 skein embroidery floss in each of the following colors: blanc neige, pink (DMC 818), blue (DMC 828), and green (DMC 504)

8 ⅜-inch buttons, ¾ inch (1.9 cm), white

8 yds (7.2 m) French val lace, ½ inch (1.3 cm)

13 inches (32.5 cm) bias binding (cut from same fabric as dress)

sewing thread to match fabric

DIRECTIONS

1 Review Construction on page 41.
2 Cut front length of fabric 49 inches (124.5 cm) long.
3 Pleat and smock the design so that it is centered. (See Figures 3-7 and 3-8.) Backsmock Rows 1 through 7 with Trellis and Rows 9–10 and 12–13 with Cable.
4 Pull out gathering threads and block.
5 Following the Design Graph, stay-stitch the neckline, armholes, and shoulder seams.

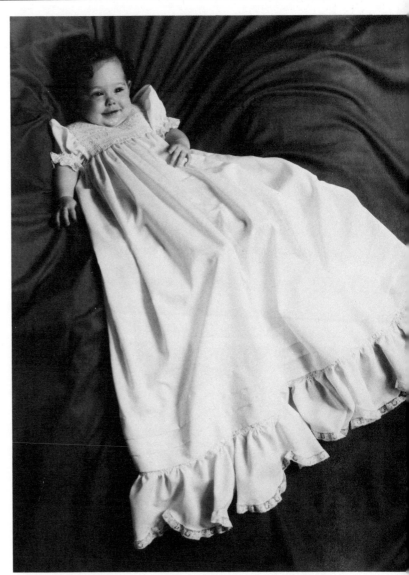

3-6 A christening gown as lovely as this is sure to become an heirloom. The Flowerette design across the front yoke is done in pastels and there is backsmocking in white. The gown was designed and stitched by Mary Leslie Sheeley.

6 Assemble the back. Stitch the back of the skirt to the yoke and make buttonholes.
7 Stitch shoulder seams.
8 Cut sleeves and roll a hem. Pleat and smock sleeves. (See Rows 12 and 13 on graph.) Attach lace edging.

3-7 Detail of christening gown design.

9 Stitch sleeves to armhole.
10 Assemble and stitch the yoke lining into place.
11 Bind the neckline.
12 Stitch side seams.
13 Make three 1½-inch (3.8 cm) tucks along the bottom of the gown.
14 Make a rolled scalloped ruffle edge. Attach lace.
15 Pleat and smock the top of the ruffle. (See Rows 12 and 13 on graph.) Pull out gathering threads. Block and attach to dress.

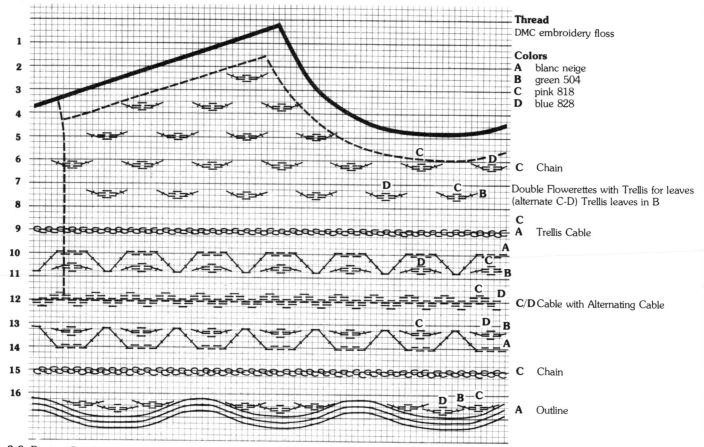

Thread
DMC embroidery floss

Colors
A blanc neige
B green 504
C pink 818
D blue 828

C Chain

Double Flowerettes with Trellis for leaves (alternate C-D) Trellis leaves in B

C
A Trellis Cable

C/D Cable with Alternating Cable

C Chain

A Outline

3-8 Design Graph.

Circular-Yoked Peasant Blouse

This blouse is fun to wear with jeans or with a skirt. It would also make an extra special gift for a mother-to-be. (See Figure 3-9 and color section.) The circular yoke was smocked in crossover rows of Trellis stitches, which create a plaid effect. The blouse was designed and stitched by Nellie Durand.

MATERIALS

> Rainbow Hill Lady's Blouse Pattern #4-1278 (see Sources in back of book) or any basic raglan pattern
> 3⅞ yds (3.4 m) soft cotton-blend fabric, white
> 1 skein embroidery floss in each of the following colors: blue (DMC 336), maroon (DMC 221), and ecru (DMC 822)
> 1 yd (.9 m) cording for tie
> 14 inches (35.6 cm) bias binding (cut from same fabric as blouse)
> sewing thread to match fabric

DIRECTIONS

1 Review Construction on page 41.
2 Cut out front, back, sleeves, and neck binding.
3 Make a rolled hem on the edge of the sleeves.
4 Mark center front. Pleat fourteen rows at top of front, back, and sleeves, and eight rows around cuffs of sleeves.
5 Stitch sleeves to the armhole edge of front and back. Stitch underarm seams.
6 Pull gathering threads so that fabric forms close pleats.
7 Smock around yoke and sleeves, leaving three center front pleats unsmocked. (See Figures 3-10 and 3-11.) The plaidlike design consists of a crossing of three rows of Trellis, three spaces high. Work each row in a different color—first blue, then ecru, then maroon. Start at Row 14. Work a

3-9 A circular-yoked peasant blouse smocked in a plaidlike design with three-ply embroidery floss, designed and stitched by Nellie Durand.

Trellis to Row 11, make an "up" Cable, and work down to Row 14. Cross over with a second Trellis, then a third. Then complete the Trellis rows between Gathering Rows 8 and 11, making sure the "down" points line up with the first row. Finish the set between Rows 5 and 8. The double band of smocking along the sleeves is two bands of the design between Rows 1 and 4. Along the neck do one band.

8   Pull out gathering threads. Block into curved shape.

9   Make the front opening and neck binding. Pull cord through neck binding.

3-10 Detail of the design in the peasant blouse.

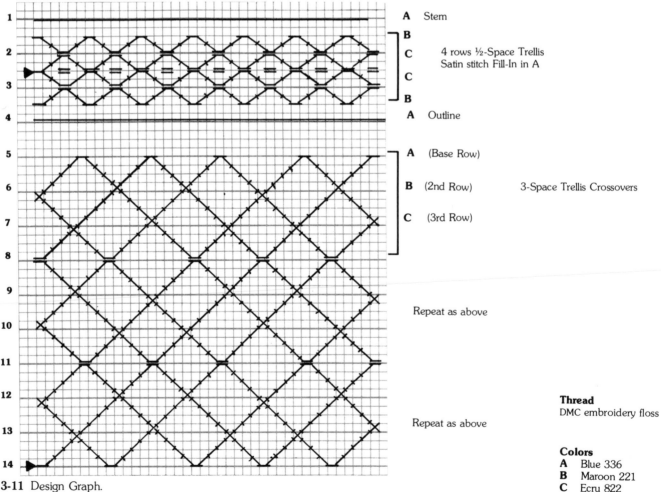

A	Stem	
B		
C	4 rows ½-Space Trellis Satin stitch Fill-In in A	
C		
B		
A	Outline	
A	(Base Row)	
B	(2nd Row)	3-Space Trellis Crossovers
C	(3rd Row)	

Repeat as above

Repeat as above

Thread
DMC embroidery floss

Colors
A   Blue 336
B   Maroon 221
C   Ecru 822

3-11 Design Graph.

Little Girl's Bishop Dress

The bishop dress is a traditional style for a little girl. As she grows taller, the dress can be worn as a blouse over pants. (See Figure 3-12.) This project, which features a round yoke, is really a toddler-sized version of a peasant blouse. The dress was designed and stitched by Dianne Durand.

MATERIALS

Rainbow Hill Bishop Dress Pattern #1-1278 or #2-1278 (sizes range from 1 through 6—see Sources) or any basic raglan sleeve pattern

2 yds (1.8 m) lightweight cotton-blend fabric, white

1 skein embroidery floss in each of the following colors: light blue (DMC 598), dark blue (DMC 517), and orange (DMC 353)

sewing thread to match fabric

3 snaps

DIRECTIONS

1   Review Construction on page 41.
2   Cut out back, front, and sleeves. Roll a hem on what is to be the sleeve ruffle.
3   Pleat eight rows around yoke and three rows on sleeve.
4   Mark center back.
5   Stitch sleeves to armhole edges of front and back. Matching all rows, stitch side seams.
6   Tie gathering threads tightly so that pleats form close pleats. Smock the design. (See Figures 3-13 and 3-14.) Smock as band on the sleeves the same as between Rows 3 and 4 on the graph.
7   Pull out gathering threads and steam into shape.
8   Make the back opening and sew on snaps.
9   Cut bias binding from fabric. Bind the neck.
10 Hem.

3-12 A lovely variation of the peasant blouse (see page 67) is this bishop dress for a little girl, designed and stitched by Dianne Durand.

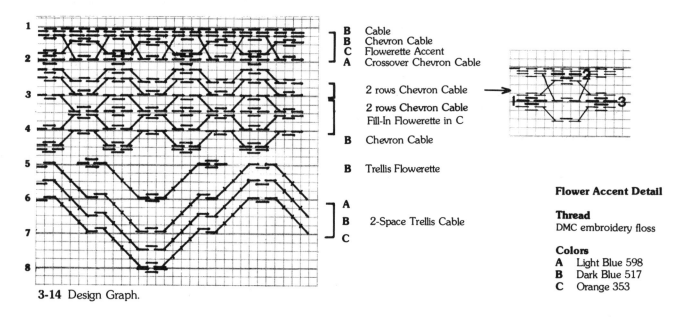

B		Cable
B		Chevron Cable
C		Flowerette Accent
A		Crossover Chevron Cable

2 rows Chevron Cable

2 rows Chevron Cable
Fill-In Flowerette in C

B Chevron Cable

B Trellis Flowerette

A	
B	2-Space Trellis Cable
C	

3-14 Design Graph.

Flower Accent Detail

Thread
DMC embroidery floss

Colors
A Light Blue 598
B Dark Blue 517
C Orange 353

Three Sundresses

These three sundresses utilize smocking in three different manners. (See Figure 3-15 and color section.)

The black sundress (Dress #1, left) has a smocked insert across the front bodice. The colors for the smocking design were inspired by the stripes in the fabric. The ruffle border along the hemline of the dress was made with the same fabric as the insert. This repeat of fabric unifies and balances the total design.

The orange sundress (Dress #2, center) uses smocking to control the fullness of the fabric around the bodice. The bodice was pleated so that the stripes of the fabric were buried in the valley between the pleats. This creates a solid background for the smocked design.

The blue sundress (Dress #3, right) has a smocked front panel. This project incorporates a border print

3-15 Each of these three pretty sundresses demonstrates a different way to use smocking and each one is simple to do.

and a smocked design that reflects the daisy motif in the border. It is also an example of how pleating is done on dotted material.

All three sundresses were designed and stitched by Nellie Durand, except for Dress #1, which was stitched by Alicia Mullins.

Dress #1

MATERIALS

Modified Rainbow Hill Sundress Pattern #24 (see Sources in back of book) or any basic sundress pattern with A-line skirt
approximately 2½ yds (2.3 m) fabric for skirt, print 1 yd (.9 m) fabric for insert and ruffle, solid
1 skein embroidery floss in each of the following colors: light coral (DMC 754), medium coral (DMC 352), dark coral (DMC 353), green (DMC 992), and blue (DMC 330)
buttons or zipper for back
sewing thread to match fabric

DIRECTIONS
1   Review Construction on page 41.
2   Cut out front insert and stitch a rolled hem along the top edge of ruffle.
3   Pleat and smock the front insert. (See Figures 3-16 and 3-17.)
4   Pull out gathering threads. Block into shape.
5   Cut out the other pieces of the garment, according to the pattern.
6   Stitch the center front skirt seam and press open.
7   Stitch the front bodice (smocked insert) to the skirt.
8   Continue to construct the garment according to pattern instructions.

3-16 Detail of Dress #1 design. The dress was designed by Nellie Durand and stitched by Alicia Mullins.

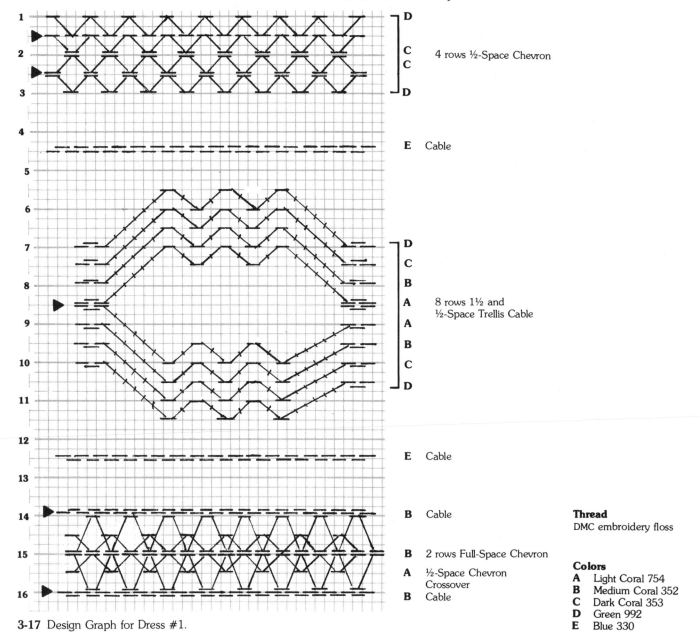

D ⎫
C ⎬ 4 rows ½-Space Chevron
C ⎪
D ⎭

E   Cable

D ⎫
C ⎪
B ⎪
A ⎬ 8 rows 1½ and
A ⎪ ½-Space Trellis Cable
B ⎪
C ⎪
D ⎭

E   Cable

B   Cable

B   2 rows Full-Space Chevron

A   ½-Space Chevron
    Crossover

B   Cable

Thread
DMC embroidery floss

Colors
A   Light Coral 754
B   Medium Coral 352
C   Dark Coral 353
D   Green 992
E   Blue 330

3-17 Design Graph for Dress #1.

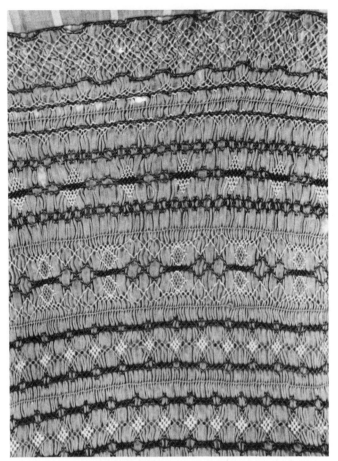

3-18 Detail of Dress #2 design. The dress was designed and stitched by Nellie Durand.

Dress #2

MATERIALS

Modified Rainbow Hill Sundress Pattern #24 (see Sources in back of book) or cut a front and back dress length, upper bands, and straps

2½ yds (2.3 m) cotton-blend fabric, striped

1 skein embroidery floss in each of the following colors: orange (DMC 947), yellow (DMC 762), and blue (DMC 796)

sewing thread to match fabric

DIRECTIONS

1   Review Construction.
2   Cut a front and back dress length.
3   Pleat front and back, making sure that stripes are in the valleys. Stitch side seams together, taking care to match each row.
4   Smock around the bodice. (See Figures 3-18 and 3-20.)
5   Make shoulder straps and attach them to top band.
6   Stitch the top band to the top of the dress.
7   Hem.

Dress #3

MATERIALS

Any sundress pattern with a fitted bodice approximately 2½ yds (2.3 m) cotton print fabric (or whatever is specified in pattern) plus allowance for front smocked panel (3 inches for every inch of finished width)

1 skein embroidery floss in each of the following colors: yellow (DMC 726), red (DMC 666), and white

sewing thread to match fabric

DIRECTIONS

1   Review Construction on page 41.
2   Cut out a front panel and pleat sixteen rows.
3   Smock the design. (See Figures 3-19 and 3-21.)

3-19 Detail of Dress #3 design. The dress was designed and stitched by Nellie Durand.

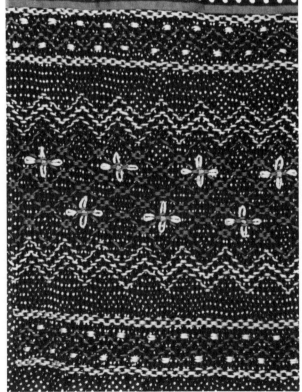

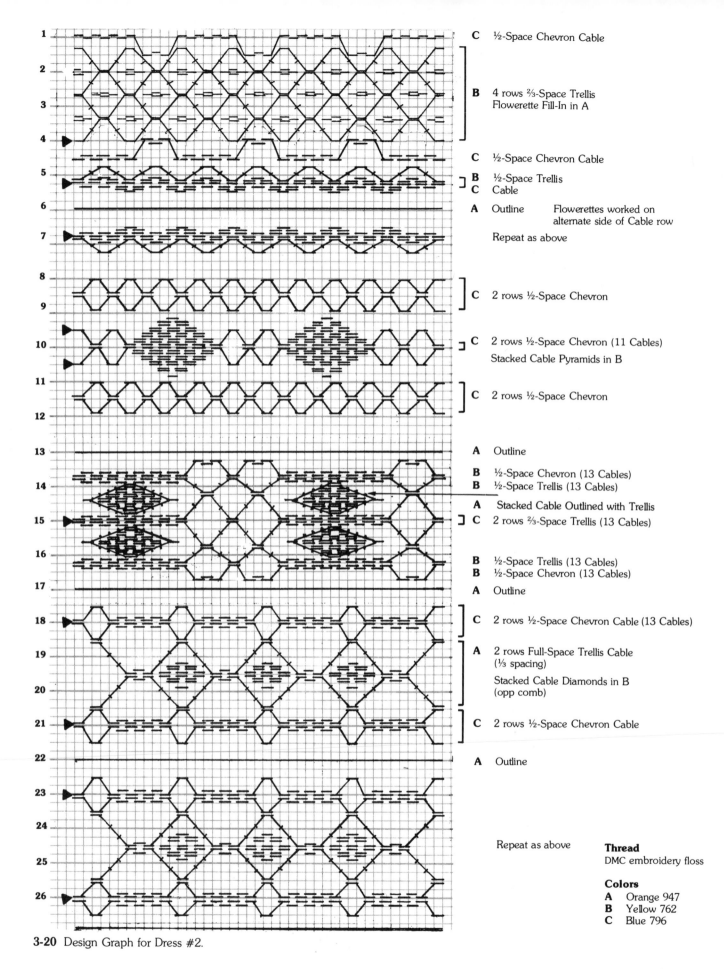

C ½-Space Chevron Cable

B 4 rows ⅔-Space Trellis
Flowerette Fill-In in A

C ½-Space Chevron Cable

B ½-Space Trellis
C Cable

A Outline   Flowerettes worked on
alternate side of Cable row

Repeat as above

C 2 rows ½-Space Chevron

C 2 rows ½-Space Chevron (11 Cables)

Stacked Cable Pyramids in B

C 2 rows ½-Space Chevron

A Outline

B ½-Space Chevron (13 Cables)
B ½-Space Trellis (13 Cables)

A Stacked Cable Outlined with Trellis

C 2 rows ⅔-Space Trellis (13 Cables)

B ½-Space Trellis (13 Cables)
B ½-Space Chevron (13 Cables)

A Outline

C 2 rows ½-Space Chevron Cable (13 Cables)

A 2 rows Full-Space Trellis Cable
(⅓ spacing)

Stacked Cable Diamonds in B
(opp comb)

C 2 rows ½-Space Chevron Cable

A Outline

Repeat as above

Thread
DMC embroidery floss

Colors
A Orange 947
B Yellow 762
C Blue 796

3-20 Design Graph for Dress #2.

74

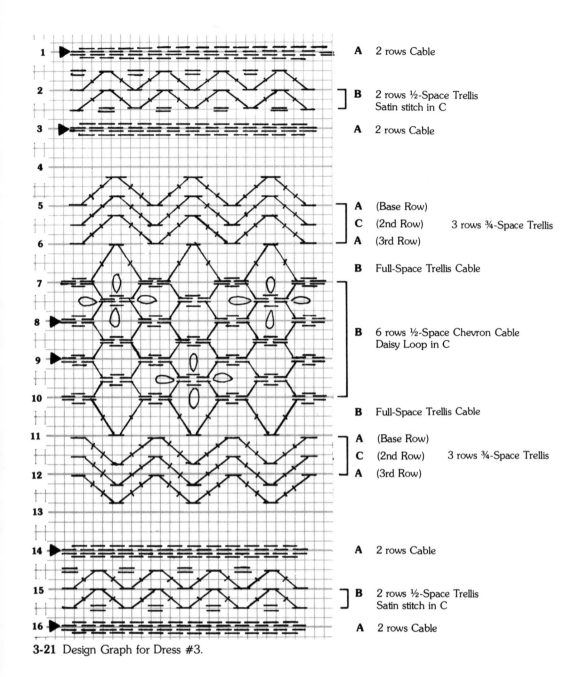

A		2 rows Cable
B		2 rows ½-Space Trellis Satin stitch in C
A		2 rows Cable
A	(Base Row)	
C	(2nd Row)	3 rows ¾-Space Trellis
A	(3rd Row)	
B		Full-Space Trellis Cable
B		6 rows ½-Space Chevron Cable Daisy Loop in C
B		Full-Space Trellis Cable
A	(Base Row)	
C	(2nd Row)	3 rows ¾-Space Trellis
A	(3rd Row)	
A		2 rows Cable
B		2 rows ½-Space Trellis Satin stitch in C
A		2 rows Cable

3-21 Design Graph for Dress #3.

Thread
DMC embroidery floss

Colors
A Yellow 726
B Red 666
C White

4 Pull out gathering threads. Block to finished width.
5 Stitch the top front band to the front panel. (See Figure 3-22.)
6 Continue the construction as specified on the pattern instructions.

3-22 The front smocked panel attached to the dress.

China-Silk Peasant Blouse

This lovely blouse was smocked in six variations of the Herringbone stitch. (See Figure 3-23 and color section.) Silk threads were used on silk fabric. The blouse was designed and stitched by Dianne Durand.

MATERIALS

    Rainbow Hill Lady's Blouse Pattern #4-1278 (see Sources in back of book) or any raglan sleeve pattern

    3⅞ yds (3.4 m) silk fabric, white

    2 skeins silk embroidery floss in each of the following colors: green and pink

    45 inches (114.3 cm) cord for tie

    sewing thread to match fabric

3-23 A China-silk blouse smocked in six variations of the Herringbone stitch with silk thread. The neck edge binding extends to become the center front ties. The blouse was designed and stitched by Dianne Durand.

3-24 Detail of blouse design.

DIRECTIONS

1 Review Construction on page 41.
2 Cut out front, back, sleeves, and neck binding.
3 Make a rolled hem on the edge of the sleeves.
4 Mark center front. Pleat thirteen rows at top of front, back, and sleeves, and eight rows around cuffs of sleeves.
5 Stitch sleeves to the armhole edge of front and back. Stitch underarm seams.
6 Pull gathering threads so that fabric forms close pleats.

7 Smock around yoke and sleeves. (See Figures 3-24 and 3-25.) Follow Rows 2 through 8 on graph for sleeves. Check to make sure each row is worked so that the pleats are pulled in "V" shapes.
8 Pull out gathering threads. Block into curved shape.
9 Make the front opening and neck binding. Pull cord through neck binding.

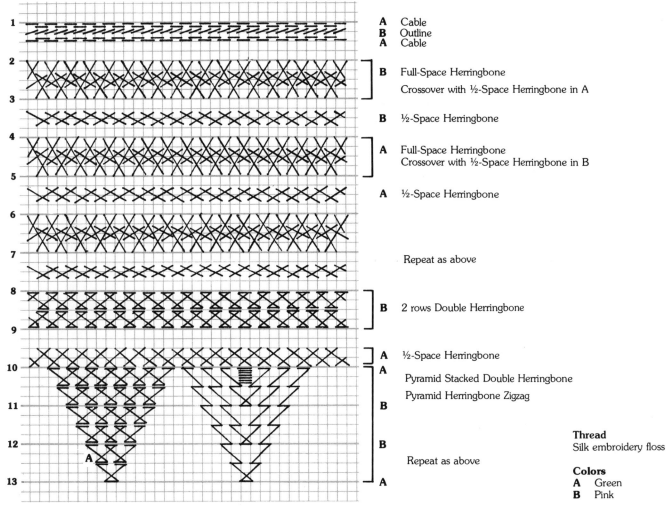

A	Cable
B	Outline
A	Cable
B	Full-Space Herringbone Crossover with ½-Space Herringbone in A
B	½-Space Herringbone
A	Full-Space Herringbone Crossover with ½-Space Herringbone in B
A	½-Space Herringbone
	Repeat as above
B	2 rows Double Herringbone
A	½-Space Herringbone
A	Pyramid Stacked Double Herringbone Pyramid Herringbone Zigzag
B	
B	
	Repeat as above
A	

Thread
Silk embroidery floss

Colors
A Green
B Pink

3-25 Design Graph.

Little Girl's "Rainbow Hill" Dress

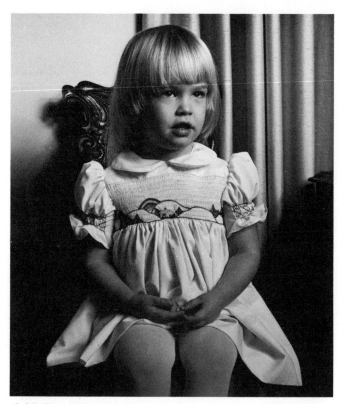

This dress style—the classic yoke—is the one most of us remember wearing as little girls. It has been the most versatile of the styles. (See Figure 3-26 and color section.) In this little dress smocking becomes a free-form scene (I call it "Rainbow Hill"), with backsmocking used to hold the pleats in the background. The dress was designed and stitched by Dianne Durand.

3-26 This little girl's dress uses the "Rainbow Hill" freeform smocking design. The background of the little scene is backsmocked. The dress was designed and stitched by Dianne Durand.

MATERIALS

    Rainbow Hill Pattern #22 (sizes range from 2 to
       4—see Sources) or any basic yoke dress pattern

    2 yds (1.8 m) lightweight cotton-blend fabric,
       white

    1 skein embroidery floss in each of the following
       colors: blue (DMC 796), blue (DMC 800), yellow
       (DMC 726), yellow (DMC 3047), red (DMC 666),
       orange (DMC 740), green (DMC 909), green
       (DMC 913), and green (DMC 934)

    sewing thread to match fabric

DIRECTIONS

1   Review Construction on page 41.
2   Cut front and back dress lengths.

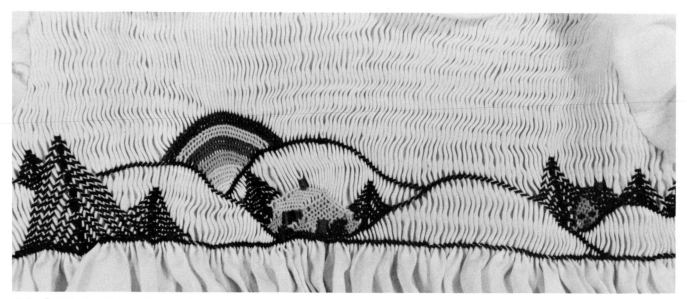

3-27 Detail of "Rainbow Hill" design.

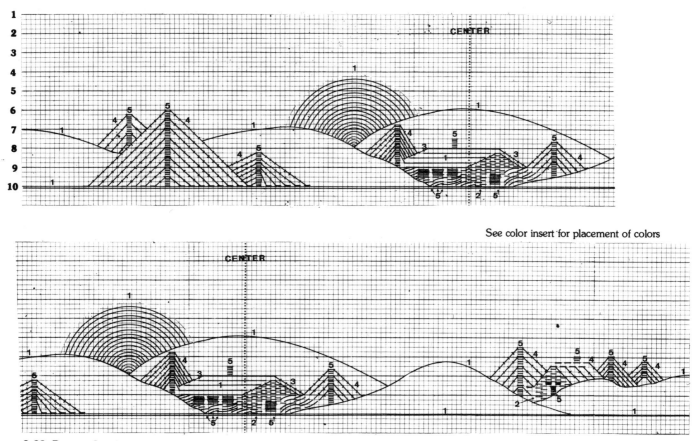

See color insert for placement of colors

3-28 Design Graph.

Stitching Chart
1   Outline
2   Stacked Cables
3   Trellis
4   Stacked Trellis
5   Satin stitch Fill-In in A
6   Backsmock with Cables on Rows 1–8

Thread
DMC embroidery floss

Colors
A   Blue 796
B   Blue 800
C   Yellow 726
D   Yellow 3047
E   Red 666
F   Orange 740
G   Green 909
H   Green 913
I   Green 934

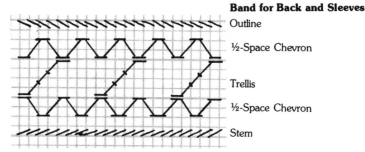

Band for Back and Sleeves
Outline
½-Space Chevron
Trellis
½-Space Chevron
Stem

3-29 Design Graph for back and sleeves. On the back of the dress backsmock on Rows 1–6. Follow the graph for Rows 7–10.

Thread
DMC embroidery floss

Colors
F   Green 934
Backsmock for Rows 1–6

3   Pleat ten rows on yoke. Smock the design on the front yoke. (See Figures 3-27 and 3-28.) For the back, leave three center back pleats unsmocked. Backsmock the first six rows or the last four rows. Smock a four-row band above the backsmocking. (See Figure 3-29.)

4   Pull out gathering threads and block.

5   Use armhole seam guide and stay-stitch along the armhole curve. Trim.

6   Make the back opening. Make the piping that goes at the top of the smocked yoke and attach yokes

to the dress. (Make your own piping by covering preshrunken cotton coil with bias fabric.)

7   Stitch shoulder seams.

8   Finish neck and collar.

9   Make a rolled hem on the ruffle edge of the sleeves. Pleat four rows and smock the band as you did for back yoke.

10   Stitch the sleeves to the yokes.

11   Stitch the side seams.

12   Hem.

Two Gingham Blouses

These two blouses each incorporate smocked inserts, but each does so in a different way. (See Figure 3-30 and color section.) Both too are examples of the use of the print of a fabric as a guide for pleating (see page 10). Both blouses were designed and stitched by Nellie Durand.

The lady's red-and-white gingham blouse (Blouse #1, left) has a vertical pleated insert running the full length of the garment. The smocked design appears at the top and waistline; the midsection and bottom were backsmocked.

The child's gingham blouse (Blouse #2, right) has a paper-doll design smocked in its insert. A smocked band, instead of elastic, was worked around the cuff of the sleeve.

Blouse #1

MATERIALS

    Any basic tailored blouse pattern

    2⅝ yds (2.4 m) gingham fabric (or whatever is specified in pattern) plus allowance for front smocked insert (3 inches for every inch of finished width), red

    1 skein embroidery floss, white

    sewing thread to match

DIRECTIONS

1   Review Construction on page 41.

2   Cut fabric for the front insert. Stitch a rolled hem along the top ruffle and lower sleeve edge. Pleat and smock. (See Figures 3-31 and 3-32.)

3   Stitch insert into the front bodice.

4   Stitch front bodice to back at shoulder seam.

5   Stitch neck facing around neck edge. Clip and press under.

6   Gather upper sleeve. Stitch sleeve to armhole and stitch side seams.

7   Hem lower edge.

3-30 Two Gingham Blouses with smocked inserts. For information about smocking on gingham see page 9. The blouses were designed and stitched by Nellie Durand.

3-31 Detail of Blouse #1 design.

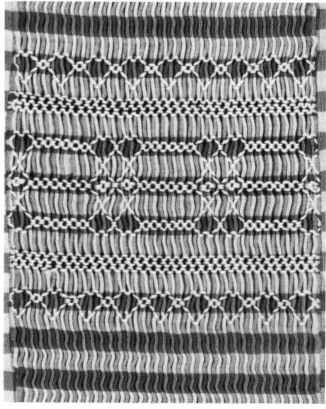

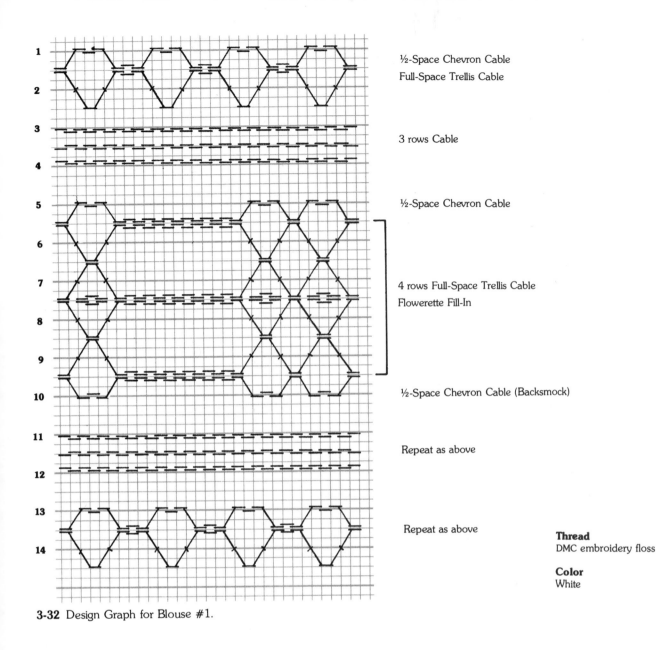

1

½-Space Chevron Cable
Full-Space Trellis Cable

2

3

3 rows Cable

4

5

½-Space Chevron Cable

6

7

4 rows Full-Space Trellis Cable
Flowerette Fill-In

8

9

10

½-Space Chevron Cable (Backsmock)

11

Repeat as above

12

13

Repeat as above

14

Thread
DMC embroidery floss

Color
White

3-32 Design Graph for Blouse #1.

Blouse #2

MATERIALS

Any basic blouse pattern

approximately 2 yds (1.8 m) gingham fabric (or whatever is specified in pattern), plus allowance for front smocked insert (3 inches for every inch of finished width), blue

⅛ yd (.1 m) lightweight cotton-polyester blend for insert, white

1 skein embroidery floss in each of the following colors: green (DMC 702), light blue (DMC 800), medium blue (DMC 799), yellow (DMC 745), pink (DMC 818), and gray (DMC 415)

sewing thread to match fabric

DIRECTIONS

1 Review Construction on page 41.
2 Cut fabric for the front insert. Stitch a rolled hem along the top ruffle. Pleat and smock. (See Figures 3-33 and 3-34.)
3 Stitch insert into front bodice.
4 Stitch front bodice to back at shoulder seam.
5 Stitch neck facing around neck edge. Clip and press under.
6 Gather upper sleeve. Stitch sleeve to armhole and stitch side seams.
7 Hem lower edge.

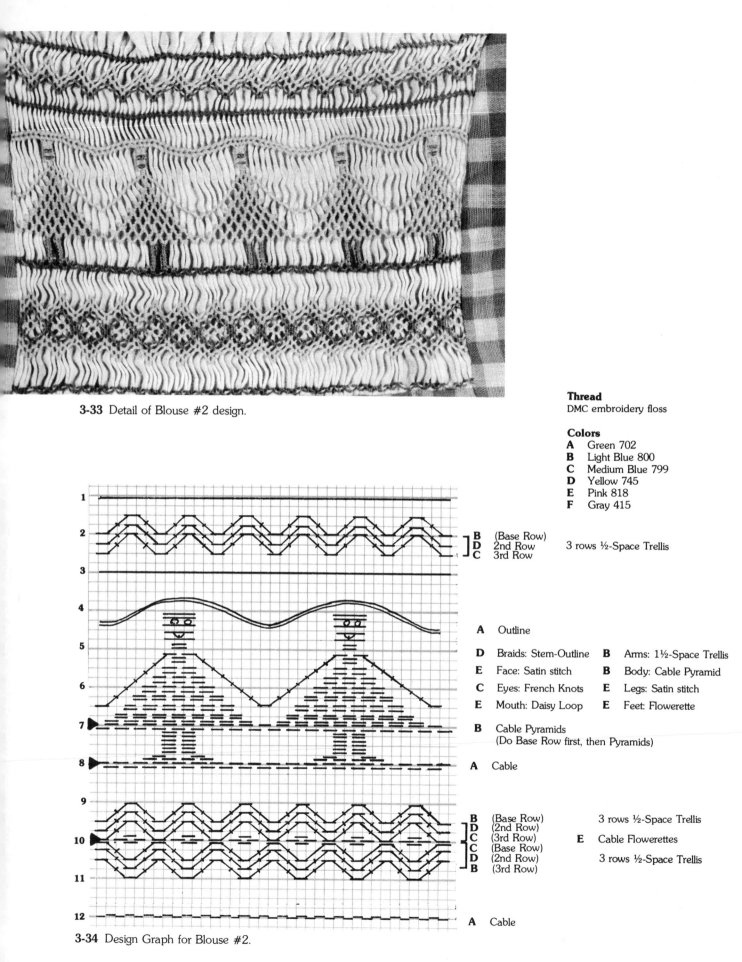

3-33 Detail of Blouse #2 design.

Thread
DMC embroidery floss

Colors
A Green 702
B Light Blue 800
C Medium Blue 799
D Yellow 745
E Pink 818
F Gray 415

B (Base Row)
D 2nd Row   3 rows ½-Space Trellis
C 3rd Row

A Outline

D Braids: Stem-Outline   B Arms: 1½-Space Trellis

E Face: Satin stitch   B Body: Cable Pyramid

C Eyes: French Knots   E Legs: Satin stitch

E Mouth: Daisy Loop   E Feet: Flowerette

B Cable Pyramids
(Do Base Row first, then Pyramids)

A Cable

B (Base Row)
D (2nd Row)   3 rows ½-Space Trellis
C (3rd Row)
C (Base Row)   E Cable Flowerettes
D (2nd Row)
B (3rd Row)   3 rows ½-Space Trellis

A Cable

3-34 Design Graph for Blouse #2.

Two-Toned Sundress

This blue-and-white sundress has a simple geometric design worked across the front bodice. (See Figure 3-35 and color section.) The dress was designed and stitched by Dianne Durand.

MATERIALS

Rainbow Hill Sundress Pattern #24 (see Sources in back of book) or any basic sundress pattern

2 yds (1.8 m) linen or cotton broadcloth fabric for dress, white

¼ yd (.2 m) soft polyester-cotton blend fabric for insert, white

¼ yd (.2 m) linen or cotton broadcloth for top bodice, blue

1 skein embroidery floss in each of the following colors: dark green (DMC 909), light green (DMC 913), blue (DMC 800), pink (DMC 223)

sewing thread to match fabric

DIRECTIONS

1 Review Construction on page 41.
2 Cut a strip 9 by 45 inches (22.9 by 114.3 cm).
3 Pleat the strip for sixteen rows.
4 Smock the design, using three strands of embroidery floss. (See Figures 3-36 and 3-37.) Pull out gathering threads and block.
5 Stitch the side bodice and top band to the insert.
6 Stitch the skirt front to the insert and bodice.
7 Stitch the back skirt to the back bodice.
8 Stitch the zipper into the back seam.
9 Stitch side seams.
10 Make shoulder straps and attach them to front and back bodice.
11 Stitch the front and back facings to front band and back bodice.
12 Make sash.
13 Hem.

3-35 A sundress in blue and white fabrics, featuring a smocked insert and long front ties. The dress was designed and stitched by Dianne Durand.

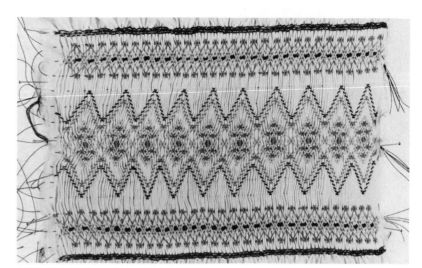

Thread
DMC embroidery floss

Colors
A   Dark Green 909
B   Light Green 913
C   Blue 800
D   Pink 223

3-36 Detail of sundress design.

3-37 Design Graph.

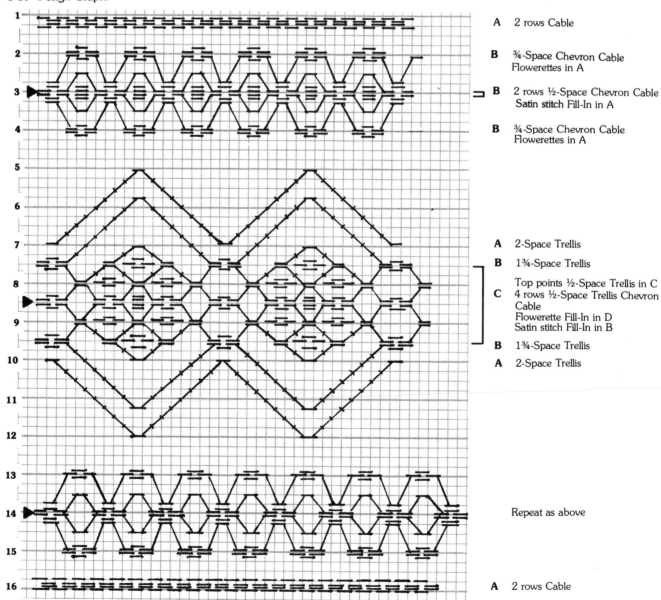

A   2 rows Cable

B   ¾-Space Chevron Cable
Flowerettes in A

B   2 rows ½-Space Chevron Cable
Satin stitch Fill-In in A

B   ¾-Space Chevron Cable
Flowerettes in A

A   2-Space Trellis

B   1¾-Space Trellis

C   Top points ½-Space Trellis in C
4 rows ½-Space Trellis Chevron
Cable
Flowerette Fill-In in D
Satin stitch Fill-In in B

B   1¾-Space Trellis

A   2-Space Trellis

Repeat as above

A   2 rows Cable

84

Two Old-Fashioned Looks

Here are two lovely echoes from the past. (See Figure 3-38 and color section.) The little girl's full-length dress (Dress #1, left) has a smocked insert with a shamrock design. The smocked bands around the "leg-of-mutton" sleeves are repeats of the motif in the insert. The long apron complements the nostalgic mood started by the sleeves. The lady's ruffled pinafore can be worn with a blouse or as a sundress. The front bodice is a simple smocked design. Both the dress and the pinafore were designed and stitched by Dianne Durand.

Little Girl's Dress

MATERIALS

    Pattern in Little Miss Muffet Designer's Workbook (see Sources in back of book) or any basic dress pattern with fitted bodice

    2½·yds (2.3 m) soft cotton or polyester-cotton blend fabric for dress, print

    2 yds (1.8 mm) fabric for insert, sleeves, and apron, white

    1 skein embroidery floss in each of the following colors: dark green (DMC 986), blue (DMC 322), light purple (DMC 554), light green (DMC 369)

    zipper, 10 inch (25.4 cm)

    ready-made piping

    sewing thread to match

DIRECTIONS

1   Review Construction on page 41.
2   Cut a strip of fabric 5 by 45 inches (12.7 cm by 114.3 cm).
3   Pleat the strip. The first row should be 1½·inches (3.8 cm) from the top edge.
4   Smock with three strands of floss. Stitch Lazy Daisies with two strands. (See Figures 3-39 and 3-40.)

3-38 These two nostalgic styles are easy to make. The little girl's dress (Dress #1 on the left) has a simple shamrock design insert. The pinafore (Dress #2) features a simple design across the bodice. Also included in the instructions are steps for making the little girl's apron. Both styles were designed and stitched by Dianne Durand.

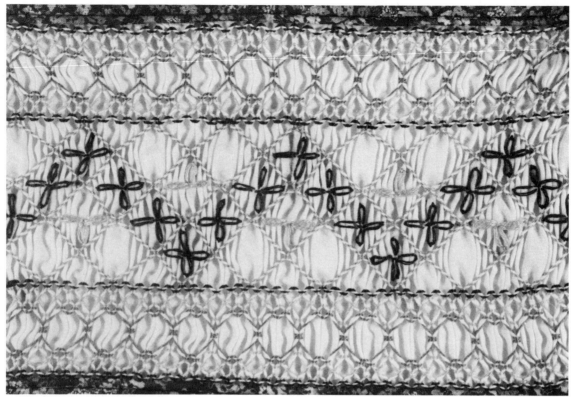

3-39 Detail of Dress #1 design.

3-40 Design Graph for Dress #1.

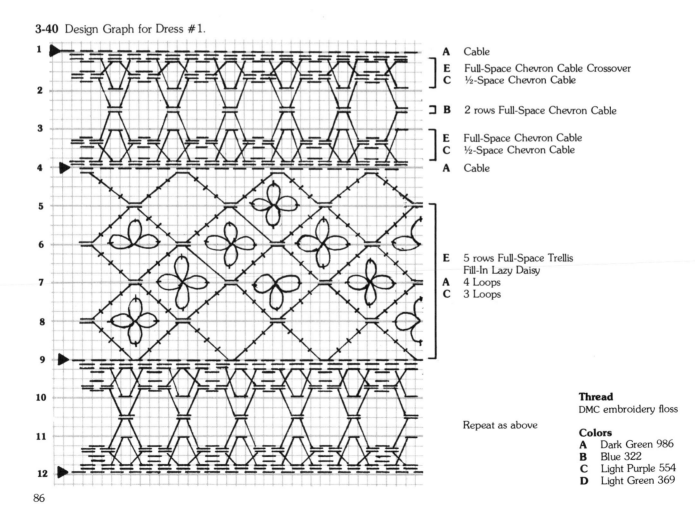

A Cable

E Full-Space Chevron Cable Crossover
C ½-Space Chevron Cable

B 2 rows Full-Space Chevron Cable

E Full-Space Chevron Cable
C ½-Space Chevron Cable

A Cable

E 5 rows Full-Space Trellis
Fill-In Lazy Daisy
A 4 Loops
C 3 Loops

Repeat as above

Thread
DMC embroidery floss

Colors
A Dark Green 986
B Blue 322
C Light Purple 554
D Light Green 369

5 Follow directions for construction of the dress.

6 To make the collar cut a strip of fabric 2 by 20 inches (5 by 76.2 cm). Make a rolled hem on the top edge and gather to fit neck curve. Stitch into place. Face with bias binding cut from the fabric of dress.

7 Adjust the pattern by adding 7 inches (17.8 cm) to the bottom sleeve length. Pleat eight rows. Stitch the design the same as between Rows 3 and 4. Work two bands for each sleeve. (For smaller sizes four rows will be enough.)

DIRECTIONS FOR APRON

1 Cut fabric for skirt 42 inches (106.7 cm) by the desired length. For the front waistband cut 5 by 16 inches (12.7 by 40.6 cm). (Shorten the length for smaller sizes.) Cut two sashes, each 5 by 45 inches (12.7 by 114.3 cm). Finish side edges with a rolled hem. To make sash points fold on the diagonal, stitch along side, and turn inside out.

2 Hem sides and bottom of skirt with a ⅝-inch (1.6 cm) hem. Fold to inside and slip sash in side seams. (See Figure 3-41.)

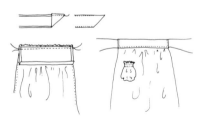

3-41 Attaching the apron band to the apron.

DIRECTIONS FOR POCKET

1 Cut out fabric for pocket from a semicircle pattern you have made yourself. Roll the top edge. Place a four-row strip of dot transfers on the fabric, with the top row 1½ inches (3.8 cm) from the top edge. Pleat. Smock the band (same as for the sleeve).

2 Gather the bottom edge of the pocket. Hand-stitch into place on apron.

Lady's Pinafore

MATERIALS

　　Rainbow Hill Sundress Pattern #26 (see Sources in back of book) or any sundress pattern with fitted bodice

　　3 yds (2.7 m) soft polyester-cotton blend fabric, white

　　1 skein embroidery floss in each of the following colors: dark green (DMC 986), blue (DMC 322), light purple (DMC 554), and dark purple (DMC 552)

　　sewing thread to match

　　1 package twill tape

　　10 buttons, ⅞-inch (2.2 cm)

DIRECTIONS

1 Review Construction on page 41.

2 Cut a strip of fabric 9 by 45 inches (22.9 by 114.3 cm).

3 Make a ⅛-inch (3 mm) rolled hem along the top ruffle of the strip.

4 Pleat the fabric. The first row should be 1½ inches (3.8 cm) from the top edge. Smock the design, using three strands of floss. (See Figures 3-42 and 3-43.)

5 Cut front waistband 8 by 2½ inches (20.3 by 6 cm). Stitch to the bottom of the smocked bib.

6 Adjust the original pattern. Stitch twill tape along the inside of the smocked panel just under the ruffle. Make sashes and stitch to front waistband. Stitch smocked panel to front side.

7 Stitch back bodice to front bodice.

8 Make skirt. Stitch front of skirt to back of skirt.

9 Stitch skirt to bodice.

10 Turn bodice back facings to inside. Turn back edge of skirt to inside to form the center back facing.

11 Make bottom ruffle and gather the upper edge.

12 Stitch ruffle to skirt.

13 Make buttonholes and sew on buttons down the back.

14 Make shoulder straps and stitch into place.

3-42 Detail of Dress #2 design.

3-43 Design Graph for Dress #2.

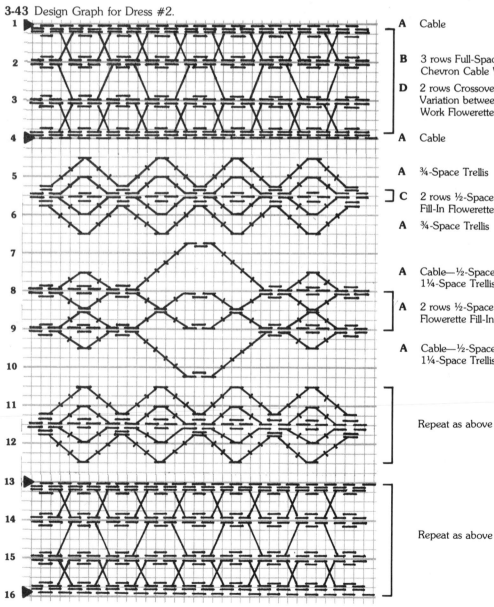

A Cable

B 3 rows Full-Space
Chevron Cable Variation

D 2 rows Crossover Chevron Cable
Variation between Threads 1−2 and 3−4
Work Flowerette Points

A Cable

A ¾-Space Trellis

C 2 rows ½-Space Trellis Cable
Fill-In Flowerette in D

A ¾-Space Trellis

A Cable—½-Space Trellis—
1¼-Space Trellis Cable

A 2 rows ½-Space Trellis Cable
Flowerette Fill-In in D

A Cable—½-Space Trellis—
1¼-Space Trellis Cable

Repeat as above

Repeat as above

Thread
DMC embroidery floss

Colors
A Dark Green 986
B Blue 322
C Light Purple 554
D Dark Purple 552

Three Evening-Out Dresses

These three elegant dresses incorporate smocking in different ways. (See Figure 3-44 and color section.) The cream-colored dress (Dress #1, left) was made of crepe de chine and smocked with silk thread. The blue dress (Dress #3, left) was also made of crepe de chine, but was smocked with gold metallic thread for a completely different look. The gray dress (Dress #2, center) was done in silver rayon thread and clear beads on jersey fabric. Dresses #1 and #2 were designed and stitched by Nellie Durand; Dress #3, by Dianne Durand.

Dress #1

MATERIALS

Rainbow Hill Lady's Blouse Pattern #4-1278 (see Sources in back of book) or any basic raglan sleeve pattern

4¾ yds (4.3 m) polyester crepe de chine fabric, cream

1 card Orizuru Japanese embroidery silk in each of the following colors: rust (98), green (731), and pale pink (96)

1 round pearl button for back opening, ½ inch (1.3 cm)

30 inches (76.2 cm) elastic for waistline

20 inches (50.8 cm) bias binding

sewing thread to match

DIRECTIONS

1 Review Construction on page 41.
2 Adapt the pattern so that the sleeves measure 22 inches (55.9 cm) across at the cuff and the blouse length equals a full-dress length in front and back.
3 Cut out to the desired size.

3-44 Three dresses for evening wear or just about any occasion. Dresses #1 and #2 were designed and stitched by Nellie Durand. Dress #3 was designed and stitched by Dianne Durand.

4 Make a rolled hem on the lower edge of the sleeves. Mark the center back.
5 Pleat sixteen rows on the front yoke, ten rows on upper sleeves, and fifteen rows on the back yoke. Pleat ten rows around sleeve cuff.
6 Stitch sleeves to armhole edge of front and back, taking care to match all rows. Pull gathering threads so that fabric forms close pleats.
7 Stitch underarm seams of garment and sleeves.
8 Smock around the yoke and sleeves, continuing to smock over the seams. (See Figures 3-45 through 3-48.) Start on the center front pleat at the "down" point of the Trellis. Work the Base Row all the way around the design. Build the rest of the design with reference to the Base Row.
9 Pull out gathering threads and block the curved yoke.

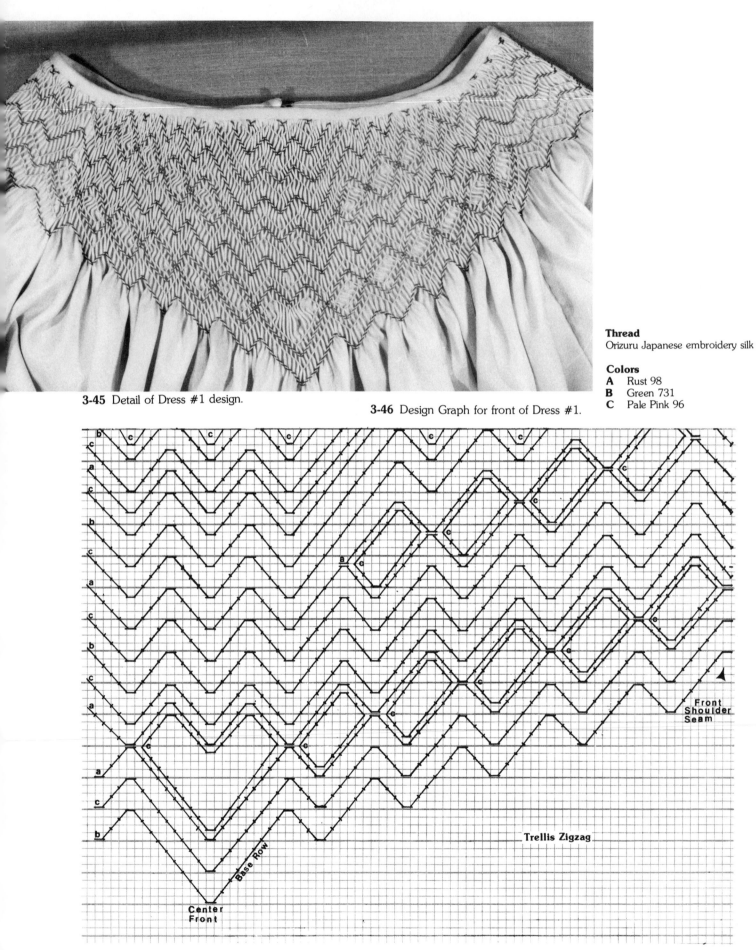

3-45 Detail of Dress #1 design.

3-46 Design Graph for front of Dress #1.

Thread
Orizuru Japanese embroidery silk

Colors
A   Rust 98
B   Green 731
C   Pale Pink 96

Front
Shoulder
Seam

Trellis Zigzag

Base Row

Center
Front

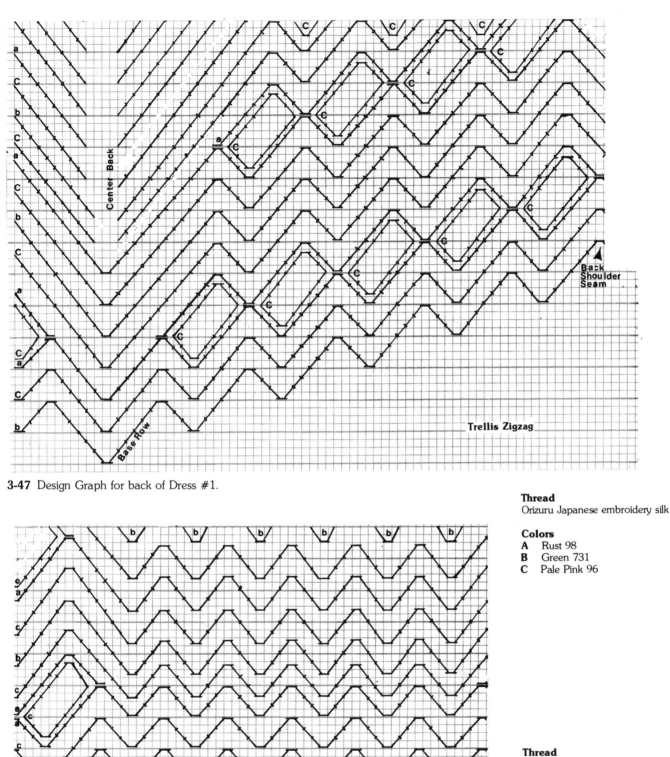

3-47 Design Graph for back of Dress #1.

Thread
Orizuru Japanese embroidery silk

Colors
A Rust 98
B Green 731
C Pale Pink 96

3-48 Design Graph for sleeve of Dress #1.

Thread
Orizuru Japanese embroidery silk

Colors
A Rust 98
B Green 731
C Pale Pink 96

10 Finish the back opening.

11 Stitch the neck binding around the neckline.

12 Stitch a bias casing around the waistline. Pull elastic through the casing and adjust to fit waist.

13 Hem.

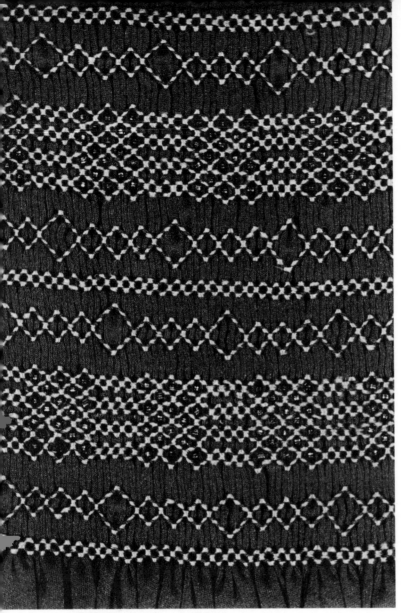

3-49 Detail of Dress #2 design.

Dress #2

MATERIALS

Rainbow Hill Chevron Dress Pattern #12-1080
    or construct the dress without a pattern
2½·yds (2.3 m) polyester jersey fabric, gray
1 skein rayon embroidery floss, silver
200 clear beads
1 spool clear nylon thread
1 yd (.9 m) twill tape, ¼ inch (6 mm) and 1 inch
    (2.5 cm)
1 yd (.9 m) bias binding, 2 inch (5 cm) and 1 inch
    (2.5 cm)
sewing thread to match

DIRECTIONS

1 Review Construction on page 41.

2 Cut one length of material equal to the front and back dress length measurements combined.

3 Mark front and back armhole curves and stay-stitch armhole curves.

4 Placing shoulder seams on center row of pattern, pleat the center with twenty-seven rows. Smock thirteen rows each for the front and back. (See Figures 3-49 and 3-50.) Work two rows of Cables on the center row for the finished width of 2 inches (5 cm) on each side. The unworked portion of that row will be the neck opening. (See Figure 3-51.)

5 Measure the circumference of your head and add 2 inches (5 cm). Cut twill tape that length.

6 Divide the measurement in half and add 1 inch (2.5 cm). Cut a 2-inch-wide bias strip for facing and place over center row, as illustrated. (See Figure 3-52.)

7 Smock area to measurement across the chest. Steam into shape. Cut out armholes ½·inch (1.27 cm) outside the stay-stitching.

8 Pin twill tape and bias strips onto dress. Machine-stitch the neck opening and clip opening along the center.

9 Turn the facing over the seam allowance and slip-stitch to the back of the pleats.

10 Stitch 1-inch (2.5 cm) bias facing and twill tape around armholes.

11 Stitch beads into place with invisible thread. Work in a vertical sequence. Tie each group separately. (See Figure 3-53.)

Dress #3

MATERIALS

(no pattern needed)
2½·yds (2.3 m) polyester crepe de chine fabric,
    blue
1 yd (.9 m) elastic, ¾-inch (19 mm)
1 yd (.9 m) cording for straps
1 spool metallic embroidery thread, gold
sewing thread to match

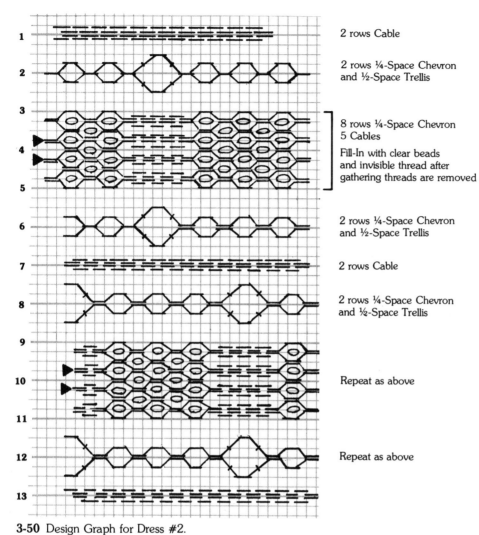

1	2 rows Cable
2	2 rows ¼-Space Chevron and ½-Space Trellis
3	8 rows ¼-Space Chevron 5 Cables
4	Fill-In with clear beads and invisible thread after gathering threads are removed
5	
6	2 rows ¼-Space Chevron and ½-Space Trellis
7	2 rows Cable
8	2 rows ¼-Space Chevron and ½-Space Trellis
9	
10	Repeat as above
11	
12	Repeat as above
13	

Thread
Silver Rayon emboidery floss

3-50 Design Graph for Dress #2.

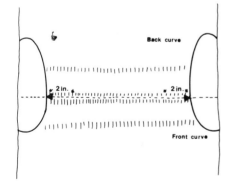

3-51 To make Dress #2, use one length of fabric equal to your front and back dress lengths. Mark armhole curves and placement of neck opening.

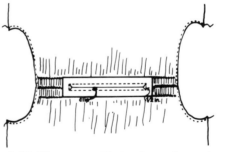

3-52 Placement of facing for neck opening.

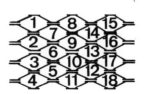

3-53 Attach the beads with invisible thread, working in a vertical sequence. (Follow the numbers given here.)

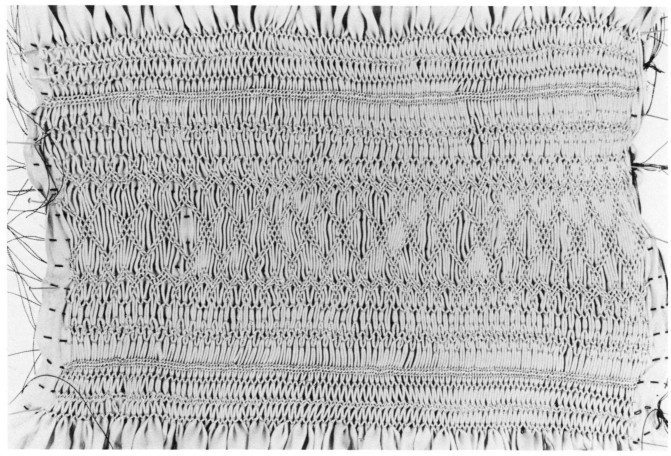

3-54 Detail of Dress #3 design.

DIRECTIONS

1 Review Construction on page 41.
2 Cut a front and back dress length of fabric.
3 Front-pleat four rows along the top and four rows 5 or 6 inches (12.7 by 15 cm) below the bustline. Measure to see what spacing you need. Work a repeat of the motif between Rows 1 and 2. Smock the design. (See Figures 3-54 and 3-55.)
4 Pull out the gathering threads. Block. Stitch the side seams.

5 Cut a strip of fabric 3¼ inches (8.3 cm) wide by the length of the chest measurement plus 2 inches (5 cm). Fold to form top dress casing.
6 Stitch a top casing around the top of the dress. Pull elastic through the casing and adjust to size. Stitch the ends together.
7 Make shoestring straps and attach to top band.
8 Hem.

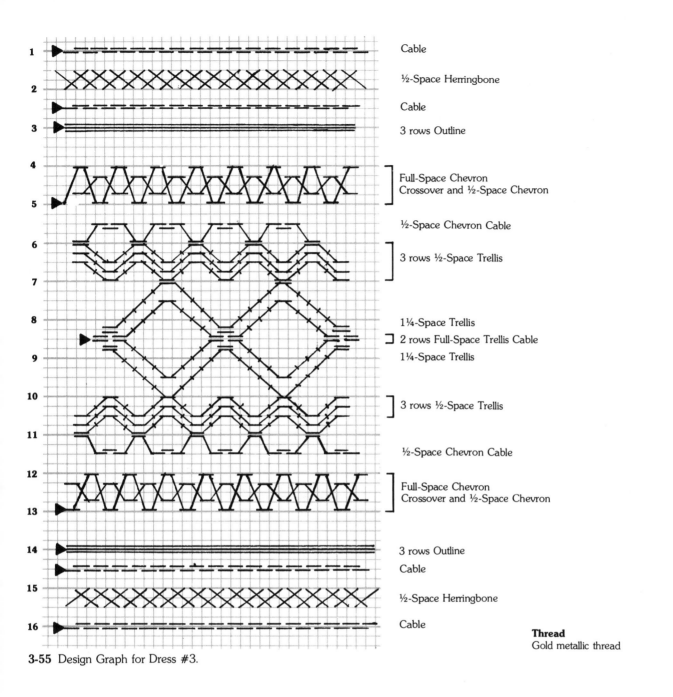

1	Cable
2	½-Space Herringbone
	Cable
3	3 rows Outline
4	Full-Space Chevron Crossover and ½-Space Chevron
5	
	½-Space Chevron Cable
6	3 rows ½-Space Trellis
7	
8	1¼-Space Trellis
	2 rows Full-Space Trellis Cable
9	1¼-Space Trellis
10	3 rows ½-Space Trellis
11	
	½-Space Chevron Cable
12	Full-Space Chevron Crossover and ½-Space Chevron
13	
14	3 rows Outline
	Cable
15	½-Space Herringbone
16	Cable

Thread
Gold metallic thread

3-55 Design Graph for Dress #3.

Father and Son Cherokee Shirts

The Cherokee shirt is a loose-fitting shirt with smocked inserts, contrasting bands, slightly dropped shoulders, wide full-length sleeves, and side slits. (See Figure 3-56 and color section.) The boy's shirt (Shirt #1, left) and the man's shirt (Shirt #2, right) are identical except for the smocking. These designs are advanced designs, which illustrate the effective use of the Trellis Zigzag. The shirts can be made out of any medium- to heavyweight cotton broadcloth, lightweight corduroy, or even a lightweight suede. Both were designed and stitched by Dianne Durand.

3-56 Father and son shirts with advanced smocking design inserts. Both shirts were designed and stitched by Dianne Durand.

Shirt #1

MATERIALS

Rainbow Hill Cherokee Shirt Pattern #11-1080
(see Sources in back of book) or any
loose-fitting shirt pattern

1⅜ yd (1.4 m) fabric for shirt (see above), cream

¼ yd (.3 m) fabric for contrasting bands, brown

½ yd (.5 m) lightweight cotton blend fabric for
insert, white

¼ yd interfacing fabric

1 skein embroidery floss in each of the following
colors: brown (DMC 433), gold (DMC 782), light
blue (DMC 798), dark blue (DMC 796), and
green (DMC 911)

sewing thread to match

DIRECTIONS

1 Review Construction on page 41.

2 Cut two strips of fabric, each 27 by 7 inches (68.6 by 17.8 cm) for inserts.

3 Pleat twelve rows on each insert.

4 Smock the design as follows: Count the pleats. Mark the center two pleats with a pin. Begin smocking on the two center pleats at the "top" point of the outside or upper Trellis. Work half of the Base Row to the outer edge of the fabric. Turn work upside down and complete the second half of the Base Row. The second row may be started at the edge of the fabric. Fill in the diamond shapes. (See Figures 3-57 and 3-58.)

5 Pull out gathering threads and block.

6 Cut out other pattern pieces.

7 Put interfacing inside front and side bands and stitch interfacing to yoke and bands.

8 Stitch entire yoke top to lower shirt.

9 Stitch shoulder seams, attach collar, and stitch sleeves to armhole.

10 Stitch side seams and side opening.

11 Hem.

Shirt #2

MATERIALS

Rainbow Hill Cherokee Shirt Pattern #10-1080
(see Sources in back of book) or any
loose-fitting shirt pattern

2⅝ yd (2.3 m) fabric for shirt (see above), cream

⅜ yd (.4 m) fabric for contrasting bands, brown

½ yd (.5 m) lightweight cotton-blend fabric for
insert, white

½ yd (.5 m) interfacing

1 skein embroidery floss in each of the following
colors: brown (DMC 433), gold (DMC 782), light
blue (DMC 798), dark blue (DMC 796), and
green (DMC 911)

sewing thread to match

DIRECTIONS

1 Review Construction on page 41.

2 Cut two strips of fabric, each 27 by 7 (68.6 by 17.8 cm) for inserts

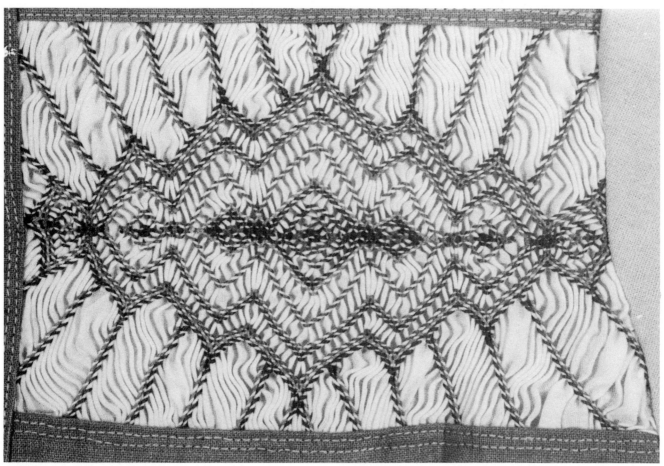

3-57 Detail of Shirt #1 design.

Thread
DMC embroidery floss

Colors
A   Brown 433
B   Gold 782
C   Light Blue 798
D   Dark Blue 796
E   Green 911

3-58 Design Graph for Shirt #1.

Trellis Zigzag with
Flowerette Fill-In

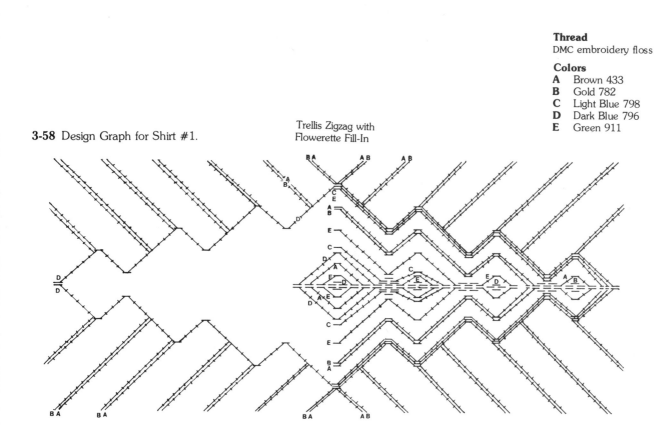

3 Pleat fourteen rows on each insert.

4 Smock the design as follows: Count the pleats. Mark the two center pleats with a pin. Begin smocking on the center of the two center pleats. The Base Rows are Trellis Zigzags. Work the fill-in shapes. These have only one Cable at the corners. Work the "top" Trellis to the "down" point. Turn work upside down, skip one pleat, then continue smocking the Trellis or Chevron. Secure floss in the back of the work before working the last Cable. (See Figures 3-59 and 3-60.)

5 Pull out gathering threads and block.

6 Cut out other pattern pieces.

7 Put interfacing inside front and side bands and stitch interfacing to yoke and bands.

8 Stitch entire yoke top to lower shirt.

9 Stitch shoulder seams, attach collar, and stitch sleeves to armhole.

10 Stitch side seams and side opening.

11 Hem.

3-59 Detail of Shirt #2 design.

Thread
DMC embroidery floss

Colors
A Brown 433
B Gold 782
C Light Blue 798
D Dark Blue 796
E Green 911

Trellis Zigzag
Thread
Flowerette Fill-In

3-60 Design Graph for Shirt #2.

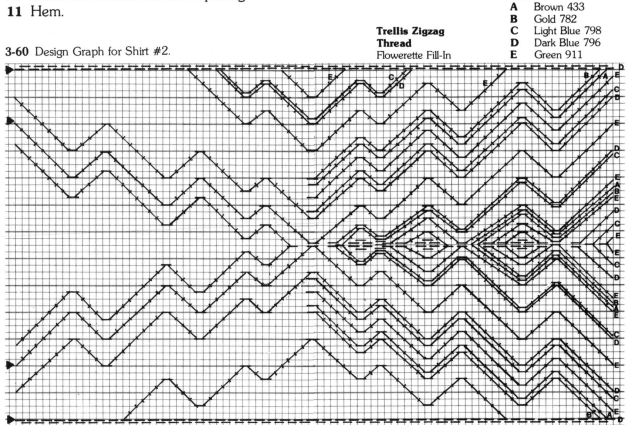

The "Susan B" Dress

This elegant dress is another classic style. The beautiful "Susan B" dress is so simple and delicate, it is a "show stopper" for any occasion. (See Figure 3-61.) The design is worked, then backsmocked. The dress was designed and stitched by Mary Leslie Sheeley.

MATERIALS

Rainbow Hill "Susan B" Dress Pattern #20 or #21 (see Sources in back of book) or any basic fitted bodice dress pattern

2½ yds (2.3 m) lightweight cotton-blend fabric, cream

1 skein embroidery floss in each of the following colors: dark green (DMC 320), light green (DMC 369), peach (DMC 353), cream (color to match fabric)

sewing thread to match

1½ yd (1.5 m) French val lace ⅝ inch (7 mm) wide

5 buttons, ½ inch (1.3 cm)

DIRECTIONS

1 Review Construction on page 41.
2 Cut two dress lengths, each the full width of the fabric.
3 Pleat enough rows to cover the full depth of the bodice.
4 Smock the design so that the top point of the Trellis on Row 7 falls on the center front pleat. (See Figures 3-62 and 3-63.) For the back yoke leave ⅝ inch (1.5 cm) unsmocked in the center back.
5 Cut out the sleeves. Roll a hem on the sleeve ruffle and smock the band, following Rows 1 through 4 on the Design Graph. Attach the lace edging.
6 Pull out gathering threads. Block front and back.
7 Stay-stitch the armholes. Baste yoke facings into place. Trim.
8 Make back opening. Stitch shoulder seams.

3-61 The elegant "Susan B" dress was designed and stitched by Mary Leslie Sheeley.

9 Bind the neck. Attach lace to neckline.
10 Stitch sleeves to front and back. Stitch side seams.
11 Hem.

3-62 Detail of "Susan B" dress design.

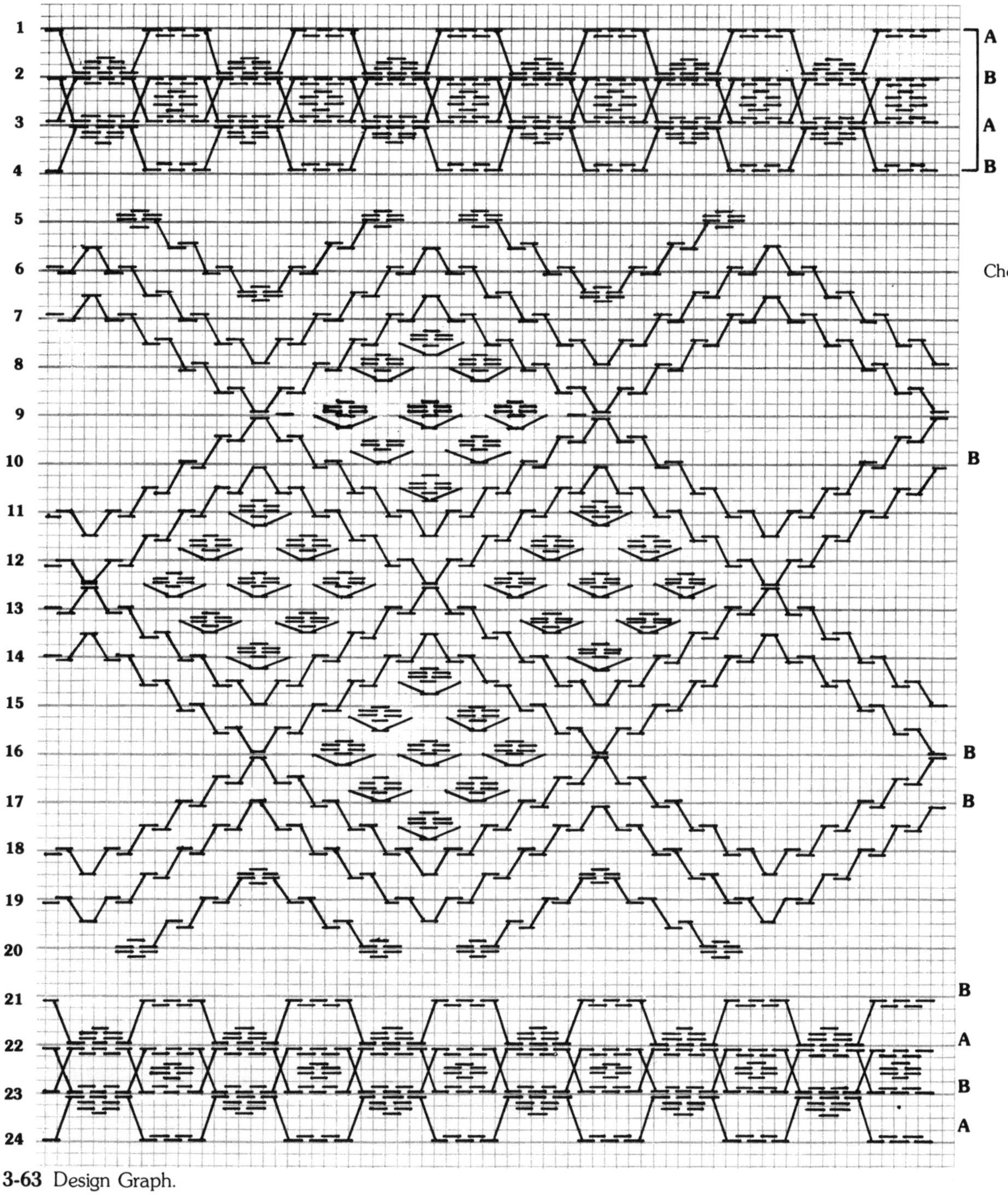
1
2
3
4
5
6
7
8
9
10
11
12
13
14
15
16
17
18
19
20
21
22
23
24
A
B
A
B
4 rows Chevron Cable
Flowerette Fill-In in C
Chevron Cable
B
B
B
B
A
B
A

3-63 Design Graph.

Thread
DMC embroidery floss

Colors
A Dark Green 320
B Light Green 369
C Peach 353
D Cream (to match fabric

Brother and Sister Jackets

These two jackets were spruced up with smocked inserts. Both the vertical insert on the boy's all-weather jacket (Jacket #1, left) and the horizontal insert on the girl's khaki rain jacket (Jacket #2, right) are simple smocked designs. (See Figure 3-64.) The girl's jacket was designed and stitched by Nellie Durand; the boy's, by Dianne Durand.

3-64 The boy's all-weather jacket in navy blue has vertical smocked inserts, while the girl's khaki rain jacket has horizontal inserts. The boy's jacket was designed and stitched by Dianne Durand; the girl's, by Nellie Durand.

Jacket #1

MATERIALS

> Butterick Pattern #5571 or Simplicity Pattern #9780 or any basic jacket pattern
>
> 2½ yds (2.3 m) all-weather fabric for jacket, navy blue
>
> 2 yds (1.8 m) quilted or flannel lining fabric
>
> 1 skein embroidery floss in each of the following colors: white, red (DMC 666), and blue (DMC 799)
>
> zipper, 12 inch (30 cm)
>
> sewing thread to match

DIRECTIONS

1 Review Construction on page 41 and adapt pattern for the insert as directed.
2 Cut two strips of fabric, each 7 by 45 inches (17.8 by 114.3 cm).

3 Pleat and smock the design, using three strands of floss. This design uses a Crossover Trellis, which creates a plaid effect. (See Figures 3-65 and 3-66.)
4 Stitch the insert to the jacket pieces.
5 Finish construction as specified by your pattern. The instructions will vary from pattern to pattern, but essentially you will stitch the front and back at shoulder seams, prepare collar and stitch it to neckline, stitch the side seams, prepare sleeves, ease-stitch upper edge of sleeve into armhole, and hem.

3-65 Detail of Jacket #1 design.

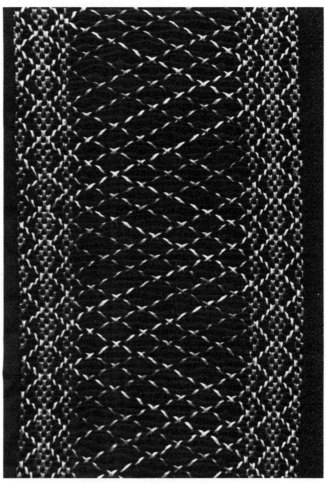

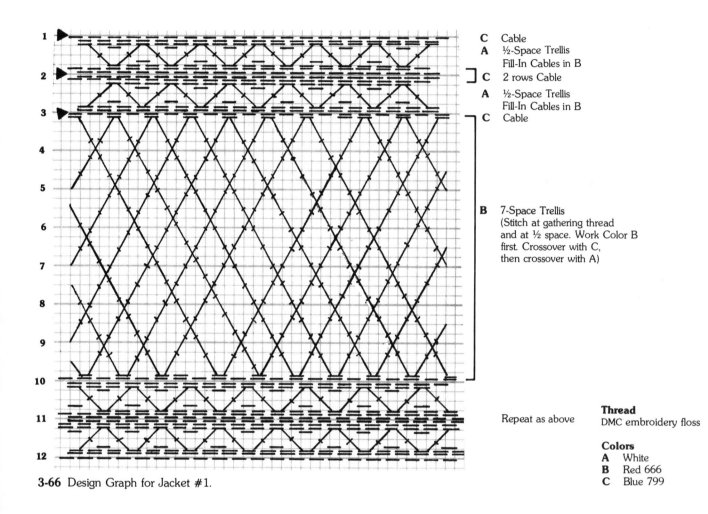

C   Cable
A   ½-Space Trellis
    Fill-In Cables in B
C   2 rows Cable
A   ½-Space Trellis
    Fill-In Cables in B
C   Cable

B   7-Space Trellis
    (Stitch at gathering thread
    and at ½ space. Work Color B
    first. Crossover with C,
    then crossover with A)

Repeat as above

Thread
DMC embroidery floss

Colors
A   White
B   Red 666
C   Blue 799

3-66 Design Graph for Jacket #1.

Jacket #2

MATERIALS
 Butterick Pattern #5571 or Simplicity Pattern
  #9780 or any basic jacket pattern
 2½ yds (2.3 m) all-weather fabric for jacket, khaki
 2 yds (1.8 m) quilted or flannel lining fabric
 1 skein #3 perle cotton in each of the following
  colors: khaki and ecru
 zipper, 12 inch (30 cm)
 sewing thread to match

DIRECTIONS
1 Review Construction on page 41 and adapt the
 pattern as directed.

2 Cut two strips of fabric, each 7 by 22 inches (17.8
 by 55.9 cm).

3 Pleat the fabric with deep pleats, using the
 dot-space method (see page 10). Smock the
 design. (See Figures 3-67 and 3-68.)

4 Stitch the insert to the jacket pieces.

5 Finish construction as specified by your pattern.
 The instructions will vary from pattern to pattern,
 but essentially you will stitch the front and back at
 shoulder seams, prepare collar and stitch it to
 neckline, stitch the side seams, prepare sleeves,
 ease-stitch upper edge of sleeve into armhole,
 and hem.

3-67 Detail of Jacket #2 design.

Thread
#3 perle cotton

Colors
A Khaki
B Ecru

3-68 Design Graph for Jacket #2.

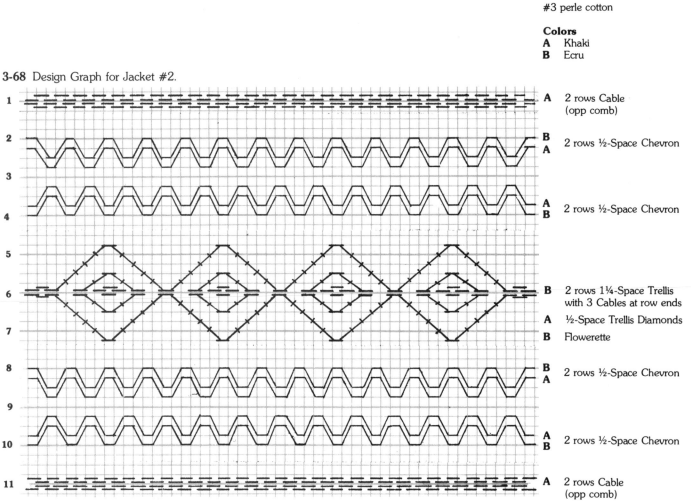

1	**A** 2 rows Cable (opp comb)
2	**B** 2 rows ½-Space Chevron **A**
3	
4	**A** 2 rows ½-Space Chevron **B**
5	
6	**B** 2 rows 1¼-Space Trellis with 3 Cables at row ends
7	**A** ½-Space Trellis Diamonds **B** Flowerette
8	**B** 2 rows ½-Space Chevron **A**
9	
10	**A** 2 rows ½-Space Chevron **B**
11	**A** 2 rows Cable (opp comb)

Chevron Dress and Shirt

In these garments the smocked bands across the shoulders control the fullness, creating a loose shirt or dress with full-length sleeves. (See Figure 3-69 and color section.) By varying the depth of the band, each project changes. Silk, organdy, voile, fine cotton, or muslin can be used. Both the shirt and the dress was designed and stitched by Dianne Durand.

Dress

MATERIALS

> Rainbow Hill Chevron Pattern #12-1080 (see Sources in back of book) or any loose-fitting caftan pattern
>
> 3 yds (2.7 m) cotton-blend or silk fabric for shirt, cream
>
> 1 skein embroidery floss, brown (DMC 838) sewing thread to match

DIRECTIONS

1 Review Construction on page 41.
2 Cut one length of material equal to the front and back shirt length measurements combined. Multiply the back shoulder width by 2½ inches (6.4 cm) for the width of fabric.
3 Mark across the center of the full width of the fabric. Mark the center front opening with a 9-inch (22.9 cm) perpendicular line. (See Figure 3-72.)
4 Pleat sixteen rows across the fabric placing more rows on the back portion of the fabric than on the front.
5 Smock the design, using three strands of floss. Do not use a tight tension. (See Figures 3-71 and 3-73.)
6 Make neck and front openings as specified in the pattern.

3-69 Both the shirt and the dress were made from the same basic pattern. The Chevron design can be adapted for either garment. Both were designed and stitched by Dianne Durand.

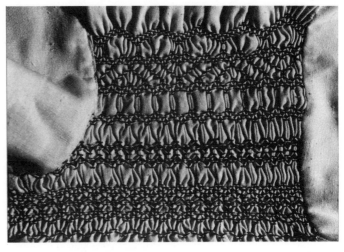

3-70 Detail of shirt design.

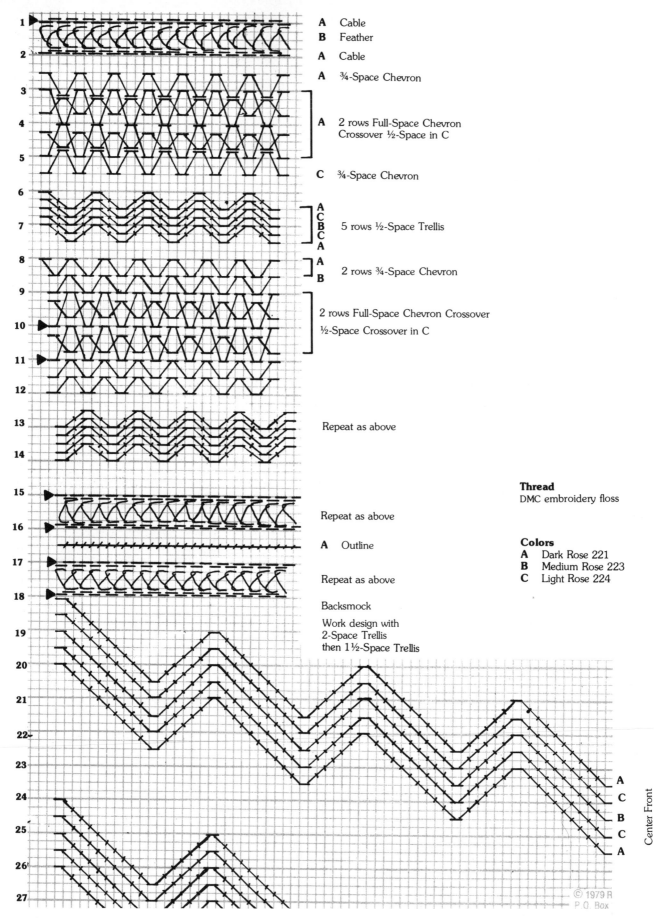

1   **A**   Cable
    B   Feather

2   **A**   Cable

    A   ¾-Space Chevron

3

4   **A**   2 rows Full-Space Chevron
        Crossover ½-Space in C

5

    C   ¾-Space Chevron

6   **A**
    C
7   **B**   5 rows ½-Space Trellis
    C
    A

8   **A**
    B   2 rows ¾-Space Chevron

9

10   2 rows Full-Space Chevron Crossover
      ½-Space Crossover in C

11

12

13   Repeat as above

14

15   Repeat as above

16

    A   Outline

17   Repeat as above

18

    Backsmock

    Work design with
    2-Space Trellis
    then 1½-Space Trellis

19

20

21

22

23

24

25

26

27

Thread
DMC embroidery floss

Colors
A   Dark Rose 221
B   Medium Rose 223
C   Light Rose 224

A
C
B
C
A

Center Front

© 1979 R
P.O. Box

3-71 Design Graph for the dress.

7 Choose style of collar and attach to neckline.

8 Stitch sleeves to armhole.

9 Stitch side seams.

10 Hem.

Shirt

MATERIALS

    Rainbow Hill Chevron Pattern #12-1080 or any
loose-fitting caftan pattern

    3¾ yds (3.4 m) fabric for dress, blue

    1 skein embroidery floss in each of the following
colors: dark rose (DMC 221), medium rose (DMC
223), and light rose (DMC 224)

    sewing thread to match

DIRECTIONS

1 Review Construction on page 41.

2 Cut one length of material equal to the front and
back dress length measurements combined.
Multiply the back shoulder width by 2½ inches
(6.4 cm) for the width of the fabric.

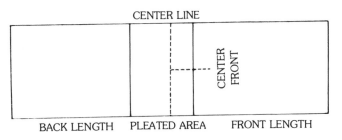

3-72 Diagram of Chevron Dress and Shirt.

3 Mark across the center of the full length of the
fabric. Mark the center front opening with a 9-inch
(22.9 cm) perpendicular line. (See Figure 3-72.)

4 Pleat thirty-two rows across the fabric with Row 17
on the center line of fabric.

5 Smock the design, using three strands of floss.
Start the front zigzag design at a "down" point of
the Trellis. (See Figures 3-70 and 3-74.)

6 Make neck and front openings as specified in the
pattern.

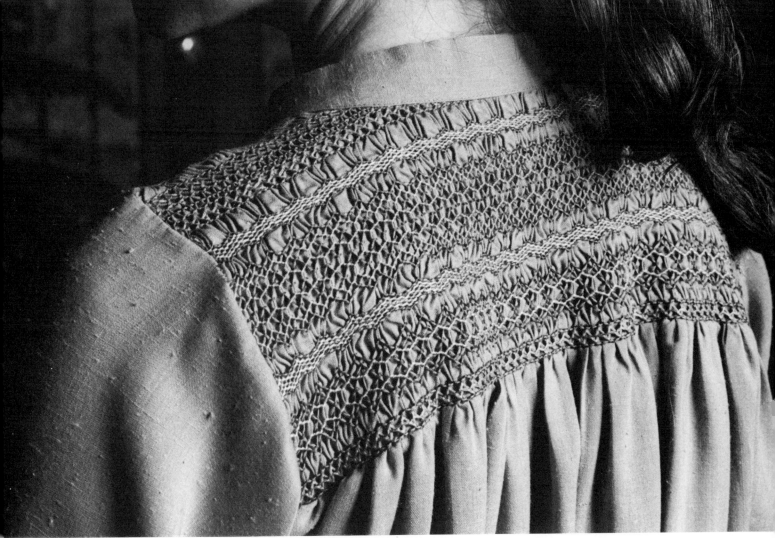

3-73 Detail of the dress back design.

7 Choose style of collar and attach to neckline.
8 Stitch sleeves to armhole.
9 Stitch side seams.
10 Hem sleeve and shirt tail.

3-74 Design Graph for shirt.

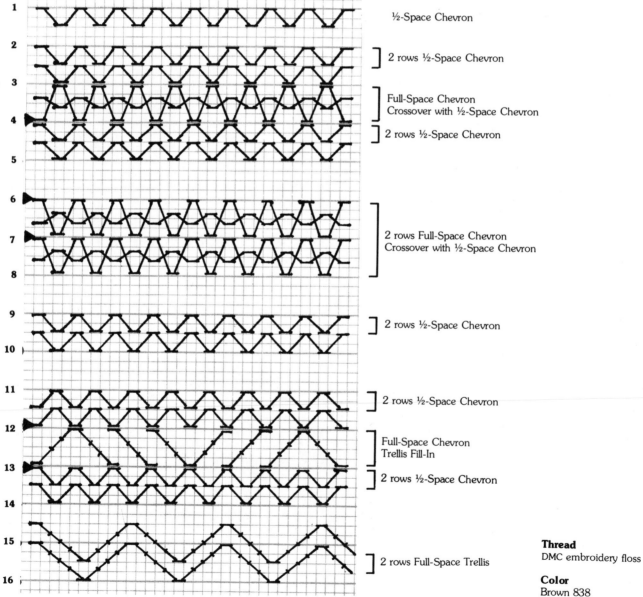

½-Space Chevron

2 rows ½-Space Chevron

Full-Space Chevron
Crossover with ½-Space Chevron

2 rows ½-Space Chevron

2 rows Full-Space Chevron
Crossover with ½-Space Chevron

2 rows ½-Space Chevron

2 rows ½-Space Chevron

Full-Space Chevron
Trellis Fill-In

2 rows ½-Space Chevron

2 rows Full-Space Trellis

Thread
DMC embroidery floss

Color
Brown 838

Little Girl's Pinafore and Bonnet

A smocked pinafore over a patchwork dress or pretty party dress creates a very special look and the bonnet adds the final touch. (See Figure 3-75.) Both were designed and stitched by Dianne Durand.

Pinafore

MATERIALS

    Rainbow Hill Pinafore and Bonnet Pattern #9-1279 (see Sources in back of book) or any basic pinafore pattern

    3 yds (2.7 m) cotton-blend fabric, white (enough for pinafore and bonnet)

    1 skein embroidery floss in each of the following colors: dark rose (DMC 221), light rose (DMC 224), and ecru (DMC 842)

    sewing thread to match

    6 buttons, ⅜ inch (1 cm) (for pinafore)

    18 inches (46 cm) ribbon, ¼ inch (6 mm) (for bonnet)

    1 yd (.9 m) ribbon, 1 inch (2.5 cm) (for bonnet)

    1 package bias binding

DIRECTIONS

1 Review Construction on page 41.
2 Take chest measurements so that three fingers fit between the tape and chest.
3 Cut pinafore front 22 to 27 inches (55.9 to 68.6 cm), depending on size of the child across the chest, and the desired length.
4 Pleat and smock ten rows.
5 Smock the design. (See Figures 3-76 and 3-77.)
6 Cut yoke facings, straps, waistbands, sash, and back skirt. The back skirt length should be the

3-75 A smocked pinafore and bonnet for a very special old-fashioned look. Both were designed and stitched by Dianne Durand.

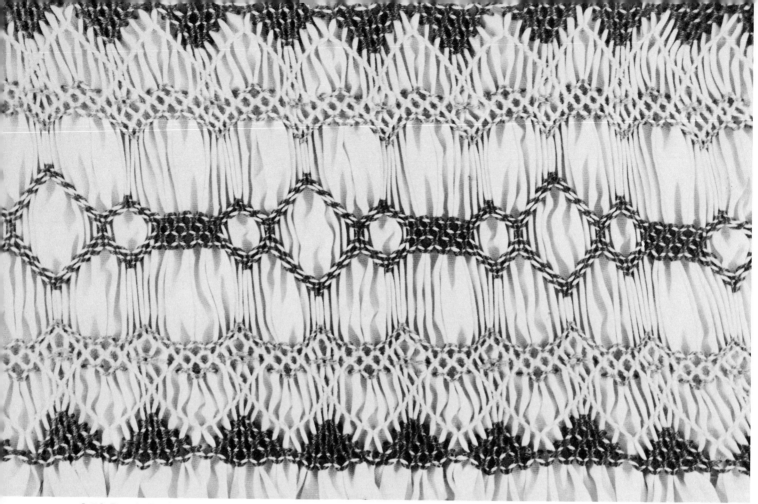

3-76 Detail of pinafore and bonnet design.

3-77 Design Graph for pinafore.

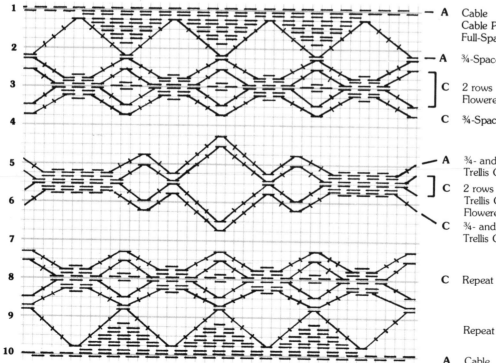

A Cable
Cable Pyramid
Full-Space Trellis in C

A ¾-Space Trellis Cable

C 2 rows ½-Space Trellis Cable
Flowerette in B

C ¾-Space Trellis Cable

A ¾- and Full-Space
Trellis Cable

C 2 rows ½- and Full-Space
Trellis Cable
Flowerette in B

C ¾- and Full-Space
Trellis Cable

C Repeat as above

Repeat as above

A Cable

Thread
DMC embroidery floss

Colors
A Dark Rose 221
B Light Rose 224
C Ecru 842

110

same length as the front panel, from the last row of smocking to the bottom, plus 1 inch (2.5 cm), and it should be 22 inches (55.9 cm) wide. The front facing should be 7½ to 9½ inches (19.1 to 24.1 cm) wide and as deep as the smocked band on the front of the pinafore plus ½ inch (1.3 cm). The width of the yoke is determined by the size of the child's chest. The sashes should be 3½ inches by 27 inches (8.9 by 68.6 cm). The waistband should be 3½ inches (8.9 cm) wide. Its length should be the chest measurement minus the width of the yoke facing plus 4 inches (10.2 cm), for ease and overlap. Divide the waistband into two bands. The straps should be 3½ inches (8.9 cm) wide and at least 16 inches (40.6 cm) long for small sizes and 17 inches (43.2 cm) or longer for larger sizes.

7 Press under 1½ inches (3.8 cm) on center back skirt for self-facing. Gather the upper edge and attach waistbands.
8 Roll edges of the sash and attach to waistbands.
9 Attach the back to the front smocked panel.
10 Make shoulder straps. Fold under and stitch ¼ inch (6 mm) around front facing. Attach straps.
11 Slip-stitch the facing to the back of smocking.
12 Sew on buttons.
13 Hem.
14 Work blanket stitch along the edge of the top ruffle.

Bonnet

MATERIALS
See Materials listed under Pinafore

DIRECTIONS
1 Review Construction on page 41.
2 Cut a strip of fabric 9 by 45 inches (22.9 by 114.3 cm).
3 Make a rolled hem along the front and side edges.
4 Pleat eight rows 1 inch (2.5 cm) from the front edge.
5 Complete the smocking design, following the Design Graph between Rows 2 and 9. (See Figures 3-76 and 3-77.) Pull out gathering threads and steam open.
6 Run two rows of machine-basting ½ inch (1.3 cm) from back edge along full width of the fabric.
7 Gather the full width to 9 inches (22.9 cm).
8 Stitch bias casing over the raw edge that has been gathered. Leave both ends open. Insert ¼ inch (6 mm) ribbon through casing. Tie in a bow.
9 Cut two 4-inch (10.2 cm) lengths of the 1-inch (2.5 cm) ribbon and form bows. Fold remaining end of the ribbon around the center of the bow to form the center section of the bow and stitch securely on each side of the bonnet. Lazy Daisies can then be worked in the center.
10 Work blanket stitch along the ruffle edges.

Curved-Yoke Rain Jacket

The smocked design on this rain jacket was fitted into a curved yoke. Topstitching accents the details of the garment. (See Figure 3-78 and color section.) This illustrates another use of the smocked insert. The jacket was designed and stitched by Kathleen A. Kiebzak.

MATERIALS
Simplicity Pattern #9592 or any other basic jacket pattern
3 yds (2.7 m) all-weather fabric for jacket, khaki
2½ yds (2.3 m) fabric for lining

3-79 Detail of jacket design.

1 skein embroidery floss in each of the following
colors: blue (DMC 798), light blue (DMC 800),
dark brown (DMC 839), light brown (DMC 436)
4 buttons, 1½·inch (3.8 cm)
thread for topstitching, brown
sewing thread to match

DIRECTIONS
1 Review Construction on page 41.
2 Adapt the pattern as instructed under inserts.
Use a fashion curve (available at most notion
counters) to draw the cutting and seamlines.
3 Cut one strip of fabric 11 by 45 inches (27.9 by
114.3 cm) for the back insert and two strips of
fabric, each 11 by 22 inches (27.9 by 55.9 cm)
for the front inserts.
4 Pleat twenty-three rows on each strip. Smock,
using three strands of embroidery floss. (See
Figures 3-79 and 3-80.)
5 Pull out gathering threads and block.
6 Stitch the side pieces to the back insert.
7 Place a pattern guide over the insert. Stay-stitch
around the outside curve. Remove pattern. Trim.
8 Stay-stitch along the seamline on bodice. Clip and
press seam allowance under.
9 Place the jacket bodice over the insert. Stitch into
place. Topstitch. Stitch front and back at shoulder
seams.
10 Prepare the front center bands. Sew on pockets.
11 Prepare color and attach to neckline according to
pattern instructions.
12 Prepare sleeves and stitch into armhole.
13 Stitch side seams.
14 Hem. Topstitch.

3-78 A rain jacket with curved front and back smocked yoke
inserts is complemented by top stitching. The jacket was designed
and stitched by Kathy Kiebzak.

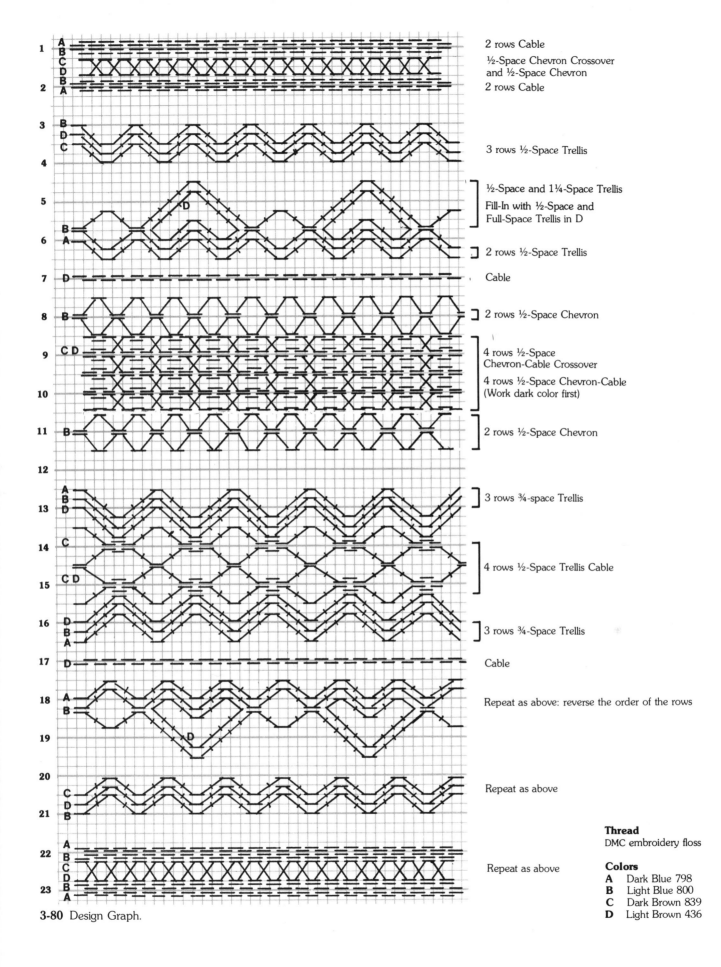

1 A B C D B A
2

2 rows Cable

½-Space Chevron Crossover
and ½-Space Chevron

2 rows Cable

3 B D C
4

3 rows ½-Space Trellis

5
D

½-Space and 1¼-Space Trellis

Fill-In with ½-Space and
Full-Space Trellis in D

6 B A

2 rows ½-Space Trellis

7 D

Cable

8 B

2 rows ½-Space Chevron

9 C D

4 rows ½-Space
Chevron-Cable Crossover

4 rows ½-Space Chevron-Cable
(Work dark color first)

10

11 B

2 rows ½-Space Chevron

12

13 A B D

3 rows ¾-space Trellis

14 C

15 C D

4 rows ½-Space Trellis Cable

16 D B A

3 rows ¾-Space Trellis

17 D

Cable

18 A B

19 D

Repeat as above: reverse the order of the rows

20 C D B
21

Repeat as above

22 A B C D B A
23

Repeat as above

Thread
DMC embroidery floss

Colors
A Dark Blue 798
B Light Blue 800
C Dark Brown 839
D Light Brown 436

3-80 Design Graph.

113

3-81 Van Dyke Zigzags, and Cables, Trellis, and Cable Pyramids make up the lovely designs on these two elegant dresses. The mulin dress on the left (Dress #1) was designed and stitched by Dianne Durand; the linen dress on the right (Dress #2), by Nellie Durand.

3-82 Detail of Dress #1 design.

Two Elegant Dresses

Both of these dresses are adaptations of traditional English smocks. (See Figure 3-81 and color section.) The dress on the left (Dress #1) is made out of a muslin fabric and is smocked with linen thread. The design consists of Van Dyke Zigzags and Cables. The dress on the right (Dress #2) is made out of linen and is smocked with Danish Flower thread. The design consists of Trellis and Cable Pyramids and is back-smocked with Trellis. Dress #1 was designed and stitched by Dianne Durand; Dress #2, by Nellie Durand.

Dress #1

MATERIALS

Little Miss Muffet Caftan Pattern (a straight band collar was used instead of the hood—*see* Sources) or any basic shirtwaist dress pattern
4 yds (3.6 m) soft muslin fabric, white
2 skeins linen embroidery thread in each of the following colors: brown, orange, and green
5 wooden buttons, ½ inch (1.3 cm)

DIRECTIONS
1   Review Construction on page 41.
2   Cut out front and back pieces. Pleat the fabric, front and back, for thirty rows. Smock front and back, leaving 1 inch (2.5 cm) in the center front unsmocked for the front opening for a front placket. (See Figures 3-82 and 3-83.)
3   Adjust the size of front and back yokes so that the bottom band of smocking will be at the waistline.
4   Stitch the yokes to the smocking.
5   Cut two strips of fabric, each the length of the front opening and each 3¼ inches (8.3 cm) wide for the front placket. Sew in front placket. Make buttons and buttonholes.
6   Stitch shoulder seams together.
7   Stitch collar into place.
8   Stitch sleeves and side seams.
9   Hem dress.

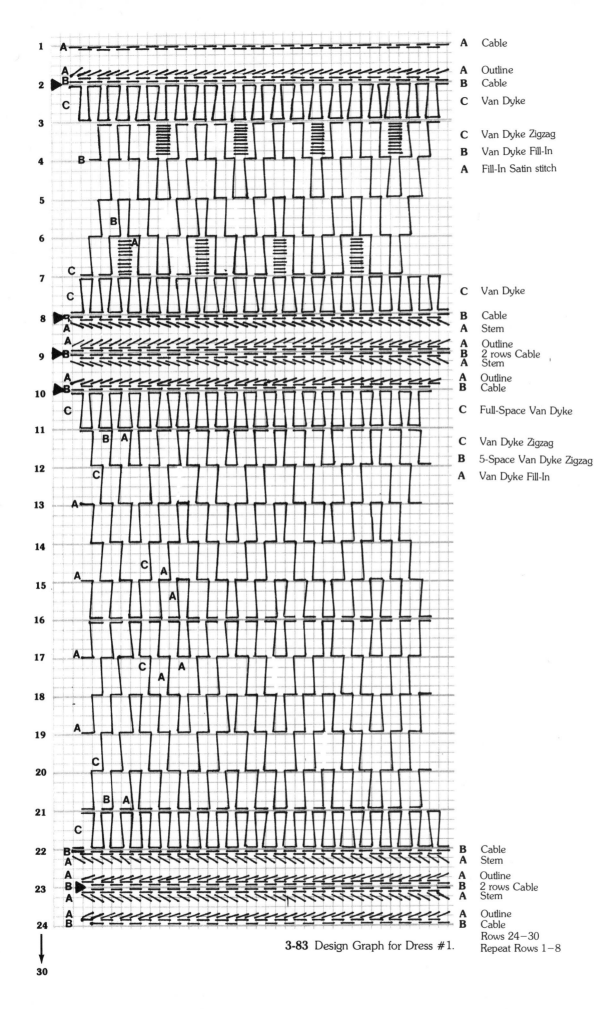

Row		Label	Stitch
1	A		Cable
2	A		Outline
	B		Cable
	C		Van Dyke
3/4	C		Van Dyke Zigzag
	B		Van Dyke Fill-In
	A		Fill-In Satin stitch
7/8	C		Van Dyke
	B		Cable
	A		Stem
9	A		Outline
	B		2 rows Cable
	A		Stem
10	A		Outline
	B		Cable
	C		Full-Space Van Dyke
11/12	C		Van Dyke Zigzag
	B		5-Space Van Dyke Zigzag
	A		Van Dyke Fill-In
22	B		Cable
	A		Stem
23	A		Outline
	B		2 rows Cable
	A		Stem
24	A		Outline
			Cable
	B		

3-83 Design Graph for Dress #1.

Rows 24–30
Repeat Rows 1–8

Thread
linen thread

Colors
A Brown
B Orange
C Green

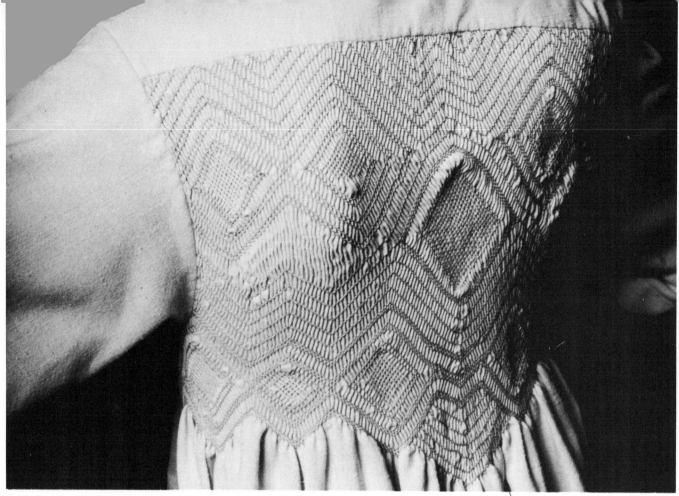

3-84 Detail of Dress #2 design.

Dress #2

MATERIALS

    Little Miss Muffet Caftan Pattern (see Sources in back of book) or any basic shirtwaist dress pattern

    4 yds (3.6 m) soft linen fabric, white

    8 skeins Danish Flower thread, in the following colors: 3 skeins light green (223), 3 skeins dark green (224), 2 skeins yellow (225)

    sewing thread to match

DIRECTIONS

1 Review Construction on page 41.

2 Cut out front and back panels.

3 Pleat front and back panels for thirty-one rows. Smock the design on front and back. (See Figures 3-84 and 3-85.) Use one strand. For the back, start on the center pleat with a "down" point of a Trellis row. Work one-half of the row, turn work upside down, and work the other half. This gives a Base Row for the design and the rest of the design can be worked with reference to this row. For the front, leave the three center pleats unsmocked down to Row 12 for the front opening. As for the back, start with the "down" point of a Trellis row at the center pleat. Work the Base Row and build the rest of the design with reference to that row. After Trellis stitches are completed, fill in with Stacked Cable Diamonds, using two strands.

4 Stay-stitch down the sides of the unsmocked pleats, forming a point at the center point. With right sides together, stitch front facing along stay-stitching. Slash and trim. Turn facing to inside and slip-stitch on inside.

5 Stitch front yokes to front panel.

6 Stitch the back yoke and yoke lining to the back panel.

7 Stitch shoulder seams.

8 Stitch hood sections together and attach at neckline.

9 Stitch sleeves to armhole edges.

10 Stitch side seams.

11 Make tucks around lower edge of sleeves and skirt of caftan.

12 Hem.

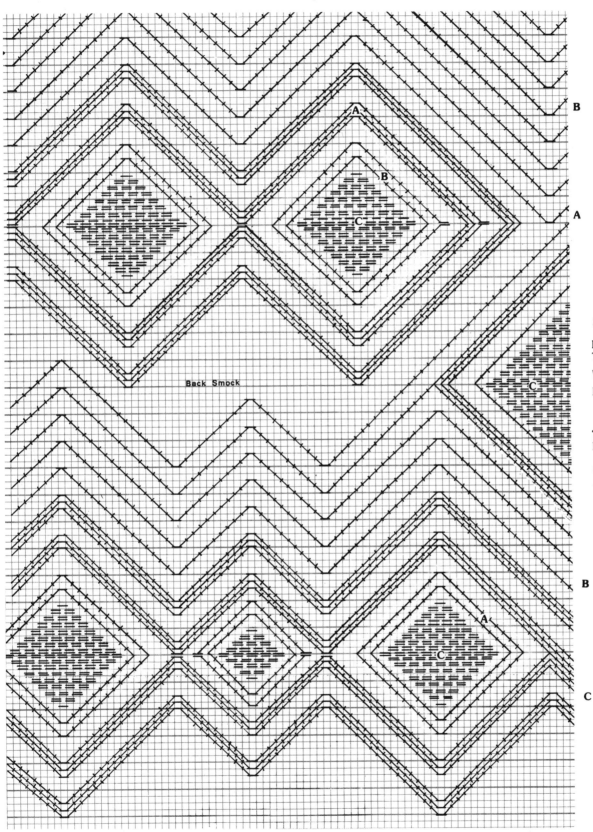

3-85

Backsmock 7 rows between
Threads 13 and 19 with Trellis

Work stitch at ¼-Space intervals

From Diamond at Center Front

Thread
Danish flower thread

Colors
A   Light Green 223
B   Dark Green 224
C   Yellow 225

3-85 Design Graph for Dress #2.

Flower-Girl and Mother-of-the-Bride Gowns

You can create beautiful dresses for the wedding party by adding functional smocking to simple gowns. (See Figure 3-86 and color section.) The flower girl's dress has a simple smocked bodice and modified leg-of-mutton sleeves. The ribbon woven in and out around the waistline and the embroidery on the collar points complete the lovely look. The mother-of-the-bride is wearing an ecru-colored silk gown smocked across the top and around the waistline and cuffs. The flower girl's dress was designed and stitched by Dianne Durand; the mother's dress, by Mary Hooks.

Dress #1

MATERIALS

    Rainbow Hill Yoke Dress Pattern #23 or #24 (see Sources in back of book), or any basic yoke dress pattern

    2 yds (1.8 m) polyester-cotton blend fabric for dress, off-white

    4 skeins embroidery floss in each of the following colors: dark rose (DMC 221), light rose (DMC 224), green (DMC 368), and tan (DMC 841)

    2 yds (1.8 m) ribbon, 2 inch (5 cm), brown

    1 yd (.9 m) piping

    sewing thread to match

    1 yd (.9 m) lace, ½-inch (1.3 cm)

DIRECTIONS

1 Review Construction on page 41.

2 Cut out the front and back dress lengths. Pleat sixteen rows on front and back, leaving a space for the ribbon. Then pleat four rows below where the ribbon will be. This is so that the fabric will be held in place by the smocking.

3-86 Two lovely out-of-the-ordinary dresses for a wedding party. The flower-girl's dress was designed and stitched by Dianne Durand. The mother-of-the-bride's dress was designed and stitched by Mary Hooks.

3 Work eight buttonholes evenly around the waistline for the ribbon. Finish the raw edges of the buttonholes by first overcasting the edge. Then work the buttonhole stitch around the opening. (See Figure 3-87.) You may use buttonhole twist or some of your embroidery floss.

4 Smock the design using three strands of embroidery floss. (See Figures 3-88 and 3-89.) Use a two-ply strand to work the Lazy Daisy and leaves. Leave the three back center pleats unsmocked.

5 Adjust the sleeve pattern by adding 7 inches (17.8 cm) to the bottom edge. Stitch a rolled hem along

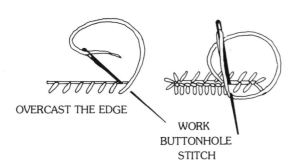

OVERCAST THE EDGE

WORK
BUTTONHOLE
STITCH

3-87 Working stitching around the buttonholes.

3-88 Detail of Dress #1 design.

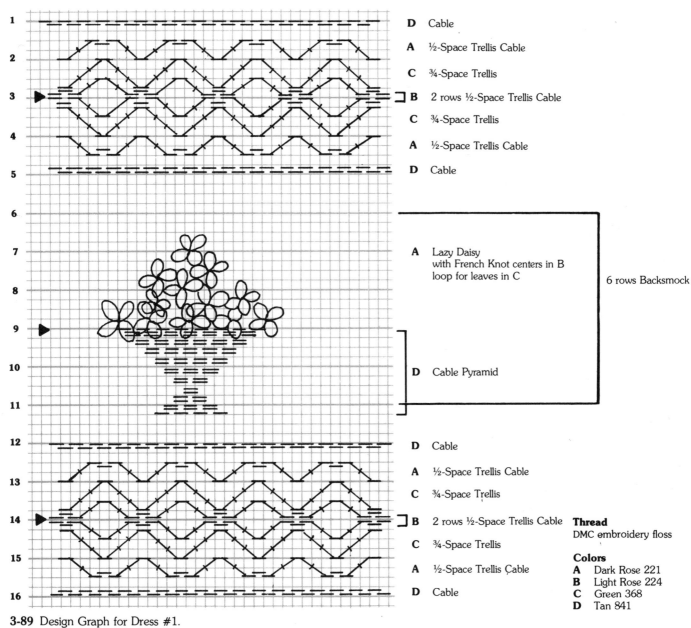

1   **D**   Cable

2   **A**   ½-Space Trellis Cable

     C   ¾-Space Trellis

3 ▶   **B**   2 rows ½-Space Trellis Cable

     C   ¾-Space Trellis

4   **A**   ½-Space Trellis Cable

5   **D**   Cable

7   **A**   Lazy Daisy
with French Knot centers in B
loop for leaves in C

     6 rows Backsmock

9 ▶

10   **D**   Cable Pyramid

11

12   **D**   Cable

13   **A**   ½-Space Trellis Cable

     C   ¾-Space Trellis

14 ▶ **B**   2 rows ½-Space Trellis Cable

     C   ¾-Space Trellis

15   **A**   ½-Space Trellis Cable

16   **D**   Cable

Thread
DMC embroidery floss

Colors
A   Dark Rose 221
B   Light Rose 224
C   Green 368
D   Tan 841

3-89 Design Graph for Dress #1.

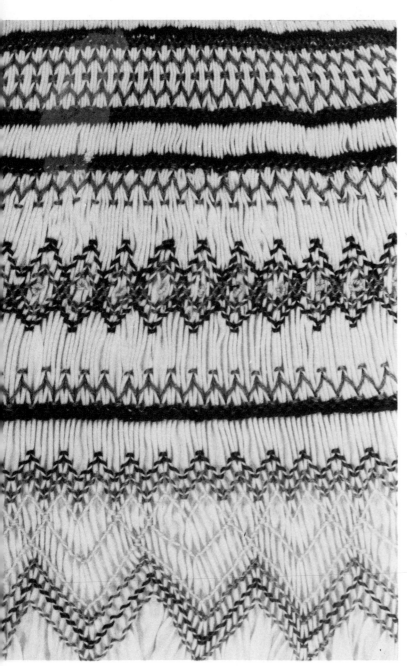

3-90 Detail of Dress #2 design.

the bottom edge and attach lace trim. Pleat five rows and smock a band 4 inches (10 cm) from bottom edge, following Rows 1 through 5 on the Design Graph.

6 Pull out gathering threads and block.
7 Follow sewing instructions as specified on page 50 and in the pattern.

Dress #2

MATERIALS

Rainbow Hill Lady's Blouse Pattern #4-1278 (see Sources in back of book) or any basic raglan sleeve pattern

6 yds (5.4 m) lightweight silk or cotton fabric for dress, ecru

2 skeins embroidery floss in each of the following colors: dark rose (DMC 221), light rose (DMC 224), green (DMC 368), and tan (DMC 841)

30 inches (76 cm) elastic

1 yd (.9 cm) bias binding

4 (or more) buttons (optional)

DIRECTIONS

1 Review Construction on page 41.
2 Cut pattern, allowing extra fabric for dress and sleeve lengths.
3 Pleat sixteen rows at neck yoke, eight rows at sleeve cuff, and seven rows at waistline.
4 Stitch armhole and side seams together.
5 Pull pleats so that the pleats are close together.
6 Working with three strands of floss, smock around the neck, cuffs, and waist. (See Figures 3-90 and 3-91.) Leave the three back center pleats unsmocked.
7 Construct the back opening.
8 Stitch the neck binding around the neck.
9 Cut two strips of fabric 1 by 24 inches (2.54 by 70 cm). Bind the lower edge of each cuff with a strip. Stitch ties so that raw edges are folded under.
10 Make a casing with bias binding and reinforce the waistline with elastic pulled through the bias casing.
11 Hem.

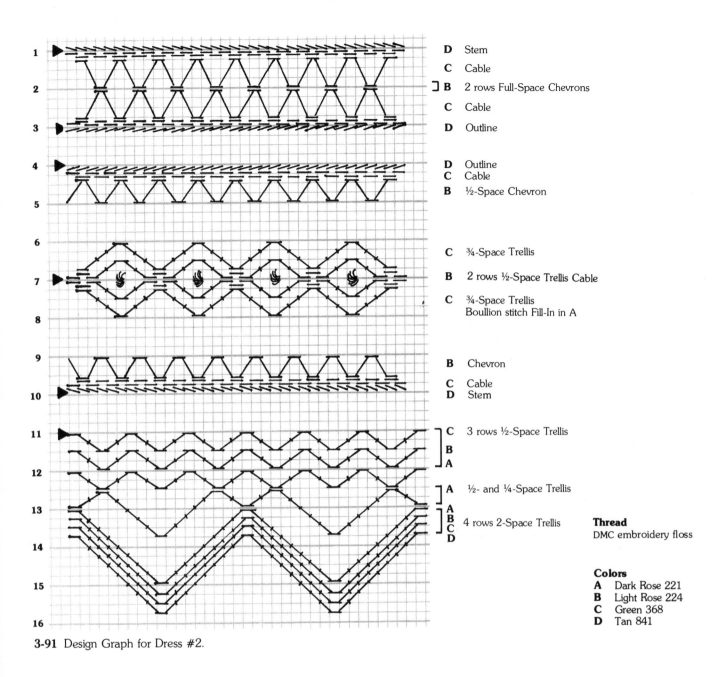

D	Stem	
C	Cable	
B	2 rows Full-Space Chevrons	
C	Cable	
D	Outline	
D	Outline	
C	Cable	
B	½-Space Chevron	
C	¾-Space Trellis	
B	2 rows ½-Space Trellis Cable	
C	¾-Space Trellis	
	Boullion stitch Fill-In in A	
B	Chevron	
C	Cable	
D	Stem	
C	3 rows ½-Space Trellis	
B		
A		
A	½- and ¼-Space Trellis	
A		
B	4 rows 2-Space Trellis	
C		
D		

Thread
DMC embroidery floss

Colors
A Dark Rose 221
B Light Rose 224
C Green 368
D Tan 841

3-91 Design Graph for Dress #2.

Two Little Girls' Blouses

Velvet is the perfect complement to these circular-yoked blouses with ruffled necklines and cuffs, but jeans might be just as much fun. (See Figure 3-92.) The blouse on the left (Blouse #1) is done in Van Dyke Pyramids, and the blouse on the right (Blouse #2) is worked with Trellis and Cable stitches. Both blouses were designed and stitched by Dianne Durand.

Blouse #1

MATERIALS
Rainbow Hill Pattern #3-1278 (sizes range from 6 to 14—see Sources) or any basic raglan sleeve pattern
1½-yd (1.4 m) cotton-blend fabric, white

3-92 Van Dyke Pyramids and Trellis and Cable stitches make up the patterns on these two circular-yoked blouses for little girls. Both were designed and stitched by Dianne Durand.

1 skein embroidery floss in each of the following colors: light blue (DMC 931), medium blue (DMC 932), dark blue (DMC 939), and tan (DMC 3032) sewing thread to match

DIRECTIONS
1 Review Construction on page 41.
2 Cut out garment.

3 Make rolled hems on the top edge of front, back, and sleeves.
4 Pleat eight rows around the yoke and four rows around the cuffs. Follow Rows 1 through 4 for the cuffs.
5 Stitch sleeves to front and back along armholes. Stitch side seams, matching all rows.
6 Pull gathering threads tightly so that fabric forms close pleats.
7 Smock the design. (See Figures 3-93 and 3-94.)
8 Pull out gathering threads and block curved shape.
9 Hem.

Blouse #2

MATERIALS
Rainbow Hill Pattern #3-1278 (sizes range from 6 to 14—see Sources) or any basic raglan sleeve pattern
1½ yd (1.4 m) cotton-blend fabric, white
1 skein embroidery floss in each of the following colors: dark green (DMC 986), light green (DMC 955), dark pink (DMC 326), and light pink (DMC 3354)
sewing thread to match

DIRECTIONS
1 Review Construction on page 41.
2 Cut out garment.
3 Make rolled hems on the top edge of front, back, and sleeves.
4 Pleat eight rows around the yoke and four rows around the cuffs. Follow Rows 1 through 4 for the cuffs.
5 Stitch sleeves to front and back along armholes. Stitch side seams, matching all rows.
6 Pull gathering threads tightly so that fabric forms close pleats.
7 Smock the design. (See Figures 3-95 and 3-96.)
8 Pull out gathering threads and block curved shape.
9 Hem.

3-93 Detail of Blouse #1 design.

3-94 Design Graph for Blouse #1.

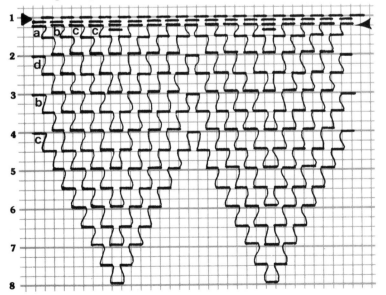

C Cable
      Van Dyke Zigzag Pyramid

C Satin stitch

Thread
DMC embroidery floss

Colors
A Light Blue 931
B Medium Blue 932
C Dark Blue 939
D Tan 3032

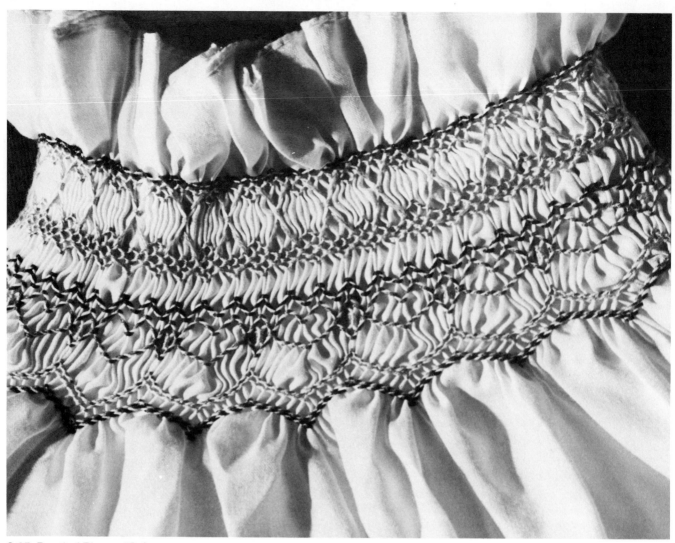

3-95 Detail of Blouse #2 design.

3-96 Design Graph for Blouse #2.

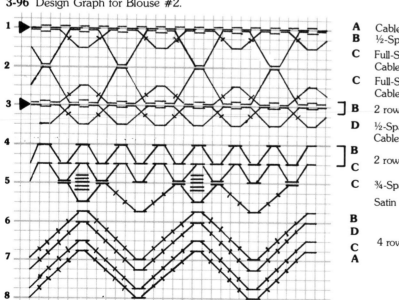

A	Cable
B	½-Space Trellis Cable
C	Full-Space Chevron Cable Crossover
C	Full-Space Chevron Cable Crossover
B	2 rows ½-Space Trellis Cable
D	½-Space Chevron Cable Crossover
B **C**	2 rows Chevron
C	¾-Space Trellis Chevron
	Satin stitch Fill-In in D
B **D** **C** **A**	4 rows 1¼-Space Trellis

Thread
DMC embroidery floss

Colors
A Dark Green 986
B Light Green 955
C Dark Pink 326
D Light Pink 3354

Hooded Caftan

This modern interpretation of the traditional English smock reflects a bright, fresh feeling with its smocked design and seam embroidery. (See Figure 3-97.) This project can be made with silk or batiste in soft pastel colors and can be used as a wedding dress. The interpretations are endless. The caftan was designed and stitched by Dianne Durand.

MATERIALS

    Little Miss Muffet Caftan Pattern or any basic yoked caftan pattern

    4 yds (3.6 m) cotton muslin fabric, white

    1 skein #8 perle cotton in each of the following colors: light blue (DMC 799), dark blue (DMC 796), and green (DMC 909)

    1 skein #5 perle cotton in each of the following colors: orange (DMC 740) and yellow (DMC 445)

    sewing thread to match

DIRECTIONS

1 Review Construction on page 41.

2 Cut two lengths of fabric, the full width of the fabric, for front and back panels.

3 Pleat thirty-two rows on each piece. Smock the design, leaving the three center pleats unsmocked, down to Row 12. (See Figures 3-98 and 3-100.) Smock all pleats along Row 13 down.

4 Cut out front facing, yokes, sleeves, and hood. Mark foldlines and embroidery lines.

5 Make front opening.

6 Stitch front and back yokes to front and back panels.

7 Stitch shoulder seams.

8 Make hood and attach to neckline.

9 Stitch sleeves to armhole.

10 Stitch underarm and side seams.

11 Work stitchery along the lower edge of yokes, down the side of smocking to stitchery line, along stitchery line, and around sleeves and hood. Work the Stem stitch and a row of buttonhole stitches on each side.

12 Work buttonhole stitch around edge of front opening. Work Stem stitch in dark blue. Work buttonhole stitch along both sides of outline stitch in green. (See Figure 3-99.)

13 Hem.

3-97 A dramatic effect is achieved with this hooded caftan, which can be made in silk or batiste. The caftan was designed and stitched by Dianne Durand.

3-98 Detail of caftan design.

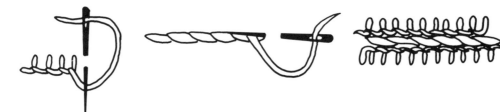

3-99 Working the buttonhole and the stem stitch around the outline.

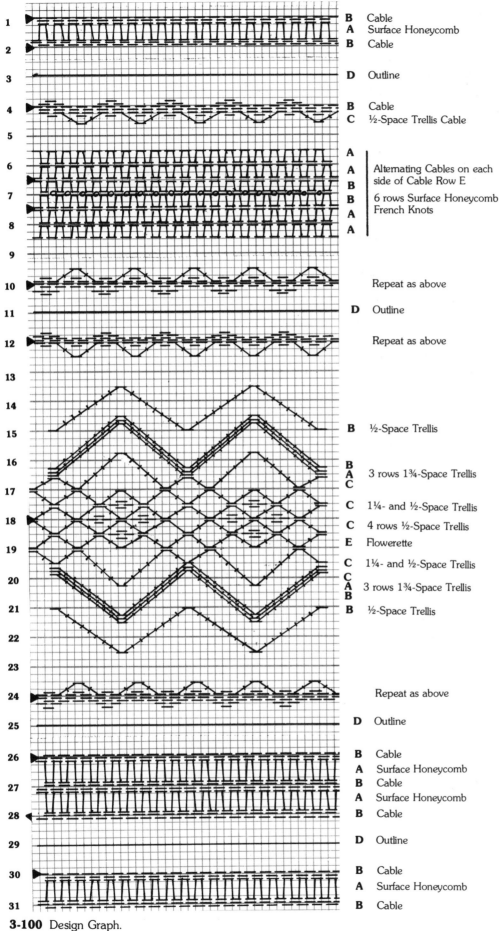

Row	Color	Stitch
1	**B**	Cable
	A	Surface Honeycomb
2	**B**	Cable
3	**D**	Outline
4	**B**	Cable
	C	½-Space Trellis Cable
6	**A**	
	A	
7	**B**	Alternating Cables on each side of Cable Row E
	B	6 rows Surface Honeycomb
8	**A**	French Knots
	A	
10		Repeat as above
11	**D**	Outline
12		Repeat as above
15	**B**	½-Space Trellis
16	**B**	
	A	3 rows 1¾-Space Trellis
17	**C**	
	C	1¼- and ½-Space Trellis
18	**C**	4 rows ½-Space Trellis
19	**E**	Flowerette
	C	1¼- and ½-Space Trellis
20	**C**	
	A	3 rows 1¾-Space Trellis
21	**B**	
	B	½-Space Trellis
24		Repeat as above
25	**D**	Outline
26	**B**	Cable
	A	Surface Honeycomb
27	**B**	Cable
	A	Surface Honeycomb
28	**B**	Cable
29	**D**	Outline
30	**B**	Cable
	A	Surface Honeycomb
31	**B**	Cable

3-100 Design Graph.

Thread
DMC embroidery floss

Colors
A Light Blue 799
B Dark Blue 796
C Green 909
D Orange 740
E Yellow 445

127

3-101 Both of these pretty dresses, designed by Mary Leslie Sheeley, are for the more expert smocker. Dress #2 (right) is a simpler version of Dress #1 (left).

3-102 Detail of Dress #1 design.

Two "Mary Leslie" Dresses

These little dresses were designed for little girls who want a "big girl" dress with lots of smocking. (See Figure 3-101.) The dress on the left (Dress #1) has a simple Honeycomb stitch on the side panels. The center panel is white to display the smocking design. This project is for the more experienced seamstress and smocker, and will be a treasured family heirloom for years to come. The dress on the right (Dress #2) is a much simpler version. Both dresses were designed and stitched by Mary Leslie Sheeley.

Dress #1

MATERIALS

Rainbow Hill Mary Leslie Dress Pattern #15-1080 or #16-1080 (sizes range from 5 to 12— see Sources) or any basic fitted bodice pattern

3 yds (2.7 m) lightweight cotton-blend fabric, solid or print

1⅛ yd (1 m) lightweight cotton-blend fabric for insert, white or cream

1 skein embroidery floss in each of the following colors: dark green (DMC 320A), medium green (DMC 368B), light green (DMC 955), dark peach (DMC 352), medium peach (DMC 353), and cream (DMC 951)

2 yds (1.8 m) piping

5 buttons, ½-inch (1.25 cm)

DIRECTIONS

1 Review Construction on page 41.
2 Cut three front panels. Pleat and smock. (See Figures 3-102 and 3-103.) The number of rows will vary with the size of the dress. Work rows of Honeycomb for side panels. Follow the graph on the center panel.

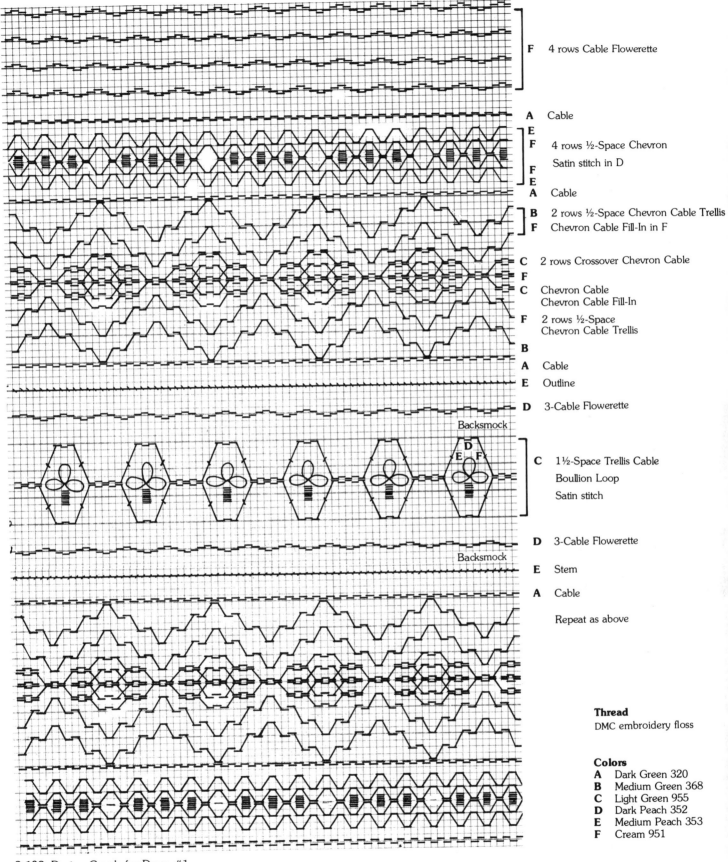

F   4 rows Cable Flowerette

A   Cable

E
F   4 rows ½-Space Chevron
    Satin stitch in D
F
E
A   Cable

B   2 rows ½-Space Chevron Cable Trellis
F   Chevron Cable Fill-In in F

C   2 rows Crossover Chevron Cable
F
C   Chevron Cable
    Chevron Cable Fill-In
F   2 rows ½-Space
    Chevron Cable Trellis
B

A   Cable

E   Outline

D   3-Cable Flowerette

Backsmock

C   1½-Space Trellis Cable
    Boullion Loop
    Satin stitch

D   3-Cable Flowerette

Backsmock

E   Stem

A   Cable

Repeat as above

Thread
DMC embroidery floss

Colors
A   Dark Green 320
B   Medium Green 368
C   Light Green 955
D   Dark Peach 352
E   Medium Peach 353
F   Cream 951

3-103 Design Graph for Dress #1.

3 Pull out gathering threads.

4 Make two lengths of piping, each the same length as the front panels. Stitch side panels to center panel with piped seams.

5 Block the front panels and place the front fitted bodice pattern over panel to use as a stitching guide. Stay-stitch around seamline of armholes, neckline, and shoulder seams.

6 Prepare bodice back. Fold back facings under.

7 Put a placket in back skirt. Stitch skirt to back bodice.

8 Stitch front and back bodice at shoulder seams.

9 Make sashes and stitch to bodice back at waistline.

10 Prepare sleeves. Roll hem on lower edge. Pleat and smock a band of 4 rows 1½ inches (3.8 cm) from lower edge. Follow Rows 1 through 4 on the graph.

11 Gather and stitch into armhole.

12 Prepare lining, using a fitted bodice pattern.

13 Baste lining to dress at neck edge. Pin at sleeve seams.

14 Bind neck edge with bias strip (the same fabric as the dress).

15 Stitch side seams.

16 Slip-stitch lining armhole seams, side seams, and waist seams.

17 Hem, make buttonholes, and sew on buttons.

Dress #2

MATERIALS

Rainbow Hill Mary Leslie Dress Pattern #15-1080 or #16-1080 (sizes range from 5 to 12—see Sources) or any basic fitted bodice pattern

2¼ yds (2.1 m) lightweight cotton-blend fabric, solid or print

1 yd (.9 m) lightweight cotton-blend fabric for insert and sleeves, white or cream

1 skein embroidery floss in each of the following colors: dark green (DMC 320), medium green (DMC 368), dark peach (DMC 352), medium peach (DMC 353), and cream (DMC 951)

sewing thread to match

DIRECTIONS

1 Review Construction on page 41.

2 Cut the front panel and sleeves.

3 Stitch a rolled hem along the top ruffle of the front panel and sleeves.

4 Pleat and smock. (See Figures 3-104 and 3-105.) The number of rows to smock will depend on the size of the dress.

5 Pull out gathering threads and block.

6 Prepare back bodice. Fold back facings under.

7 Stitch front and back bodice at shoulder seams.

8 Prepare sleeves the same as in Dress #1.

9 Stitch side bodice seams.

10 Gather the top of the skirt and pin to front and back bodice, distributing the fullness evenly. Stitch and trim.

11 Prepare a belt 1¼ inches (3.2 cm) wide and 14 inches (35.5 cm) long. Stitch to dress at waist.

12 Prepare two bias strips 2¼ inches (5.6 cm) wide and the total length of the back neckline, front bodice, and skirt. Fold lengthwise and press gently.

13 Pin bias strip to right side of garment around the neck edge, down the front bodice, and skirt.

14 Slip-stitch bias strip over seams.

15 Pin side panels of dress over smocked front panel. The bottom row should be at the waistline.

16 Stitch close to the bias binding.

17 Finish back skirt seam. With right sides together, place edge of left skirt 1¼ inch (3 cm) from edge of right skirt. Beginning 4 inches (10 cm) below waistline, pin and baste 1¼ inch (3 cm) from edge of right skirt. Stitch to bottom of skirt. Stitch across top of placket ½ inch (3.8 cm). Press seam to the right side of garment. Fold left back facing to the left of garment 1¼ inch (3 cm). Make buttonholes. Sew on buttons. Hem.

3-104 Detail of Dress #2 design.

Thread
DMC embroidery floss

Colors
A Dark Green 320
B Medium Green 368
C Pale Peach 352
D Medium Peach 353
E Cream 951

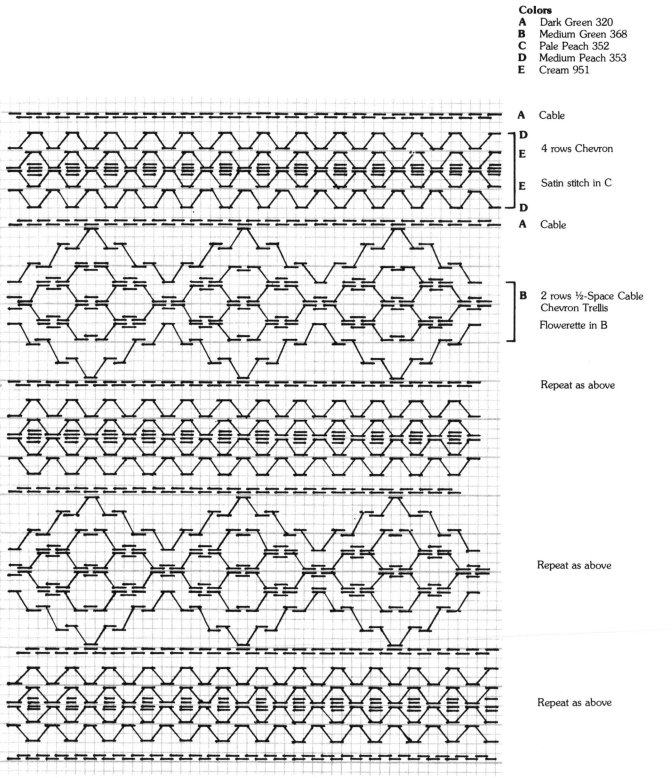

A Cable

D
E 4 rows Chevron

E Satin stitch in C
D

A Cable

B 2 rows ½-Space Cable
Chevron Trellis

Flowerette in B

Repeat as above

Repeat as above

Repeat as above

3-105 Design Graph for Dress #2.

GLOSSARY
OF SMOCKING

Analogous Colors: colors that are next to each other on a color wheel.

Baby Wave (Half-Space Chevron stitch, Diamond stitch): modified Cable stitch. The height may vary from one-quarter to full space.

Baby Diamond: two rows of Half-Space Chevron stitch. Two pleats will be in the center of each diamond.

Backsmocking: Cable or Trellis rows worked on the wrong side of the pleats. The thread is always matched to the fabric. Backsmocking is used to hold pleats in place where there is to be no smocking on the front, to create a "shadow" effect on the face of the work, and to balance the tension so that a ruffle will stand up straight. Backsmocking will give added control to the fullness of fabric, such as around cuffs and neck ruffles.

Bars: Satin stitch over two pleats.

Base Row: the row of a design that should be worked first. This row is a reference for the other rows, which may be worked on either side of the base row.

Braid: adjacent rows of Outline and Stem stitch.

Cable Stitch (Level stitch, the "basic stitch"): a Straight stitch with many uses, such as for backsmocking, for borders, for base rows in designs, for aligning pleats, and for building shapes. It is a close stitch and should not be used along the bottom of round yokes where a loose flare is needed.

Chevron Design: Zigzag stitches worked to form a wave design.

Chevron Stitch (Baby Wave, Diamond): a modified Cable, forming a Zigzag stitch between the gathering threads. The height may vary from one-quarter to full space.

Complementary Colors: colors directly opposite each other on the color wheel.

Cool Colors: blues, greens, and purples. These colors seem to recede and appear smaller.

Daisy (Daisy Chain stitch): embroidery loops worked to form a flower shape. They are usually worked in clusters to form bouquets or single shapes to add detail to a design.

Diamond: rows of opposite Zigzag stitches, usually the Chevron, Surface Honeycomb, and Trellis.

Discordant Colors: colors of different tonal values.

Double Flowerette: six Cable stitches worked over four pleats to form a small flower shape. It is used to decorate the inside of diamonds and lattices.

Feather Stitch: an embroidery stitch with several variations. It is worked from right to left, with two pleats picked up at once, one old pleat and one new one. There are a number of variations and the elasticity will vary. It is worked in a freeform manner to form clouds or as a Straight stitch to form a solid band of color in a design.

Fill-In Stitches: embroidery stitches worked after the design has been completed. These accent and add detail to a design. They are nonelastic stitches. Care must be taken when going from position to position so that the elasticity of the total piece is not affected.

Fill-In Technique: the method of working series of stitches that are not a continuous row.

Flowerette: four Cables worked across four pleats form a small flower. It is used to accent and add detail to a design.

Gathering Thread (gathering line, guidelines, pleating lines, basting threads): threads used to gather pleats, which also serve as guides for rows of smocking.

Herringbone: a Zigzag stitch that makes interesting pleat patterns. It is worked from left to right, with two pleats picked up at once, an old and a new pleat.

Honeycomb: the most elastic stitch that holds the pleats in effective shapes. The thread passes behind the pleats in a zigzag manner.

Hue: the pure state of color—red, orange, yellow, green, blue, indigo, violet.

Intensity or Saturation: refers to the brightness or dullness of a color.

Large Wave: Full-Space Trellis, Four-Step Wave, or Chevron.

Lattice: several rows of Zigzag stitches. It is used as background for Fill-In stitches.

Mock Chain (Wheat stitch): adjacent rows of Outline and Stem stitches.

Opposite Rows: rows where the top stitches fall across the same pleats as the bottom stitches of the adjacent row, used to create shapes such as diamonds, lattices, and pyramids.

Outline Stitch: a Straight stitch worked with the thread held above the needle. It is used to add color in a small area and as a border for many designs. This is a close stitch and should not be used where a loose flare is needed.

Parallel Rows: rows where the top and bottom stitches fall across the same pleats, used to make lines, waves, and square shapes.

Pleater (smock gathering machine): a machine that will pleat fabric and run the gathering thread through the pleats at the same time.

Pleats (reeds, tubes): gathers of the fabric.

Primary Colors: colors that cannot be obtained from other colors—red, yellow, and blue.

Quarter Wave: Half-Space Trellis, Two-Step Wave, or Chevron.

Row (stitch row, design row, horizontal row of smocking): one continuous series of stitches.

Satin Stitch: several stitches worked across two or more pleats forming a solid block of color. It is used to fill in and to add accent color in a design.

Secondary Colors: colors obtained from the mixture of equal proportions of two primary colors—orange, green, purple.

Seed Stitch (Dot): two Satin stitches over two pleats. It is used to fill in a Chevron Diamond.

Simple Wave: a Two-Step Trellis worked over a full space.

Space: the area between two gathering threads.

Spools: Satin stitches worked over four pleats.

Stacked Cables (Cable Pyramids, Cable Shapes, Weaving, Basket stitch, Triangles): the process of smocking rows of cables at one-quarter-space intervals either opposite or parallel to each other.

Stem Stitch: a Straight stitch worked with the thread held below the needle. It is used as a border for designs and to add color in a small space. This is a close stitch and should not be used where a loose flare is needed.

Straight Stitches: those stitches that are worked straight across the pleats following the gathering threads. (Outline, Stem, Cable, Chain, Raised Chain)

Surface Honeycomb: a Zigzag stitch similar to the Chevron, but the needle works through the same pleat twice. Opposite rows form diamonds without pleats in the center.

Tertiary Colors: a group of six variations obtained by mixing a primary color with the adjacent secondary color.

Transfer Dots (smocking spots): sheets of dots used as guides for the gathering threads. These are applied to the wrong side of the fabric with a warm iron and will be washed out after fabric is pleated.

Trellis: a Zigzag stitch that is a combination of Bottom Cable, Stem stitch, a Top Cable, and Outline stitch. It may be worked to various heights at intervals of one-half, one-third, one-quarter, one-fifth, etc. This stitch or a combination of it is used where elasticity is needed, such as at the bottom of round yokes.

Turret: Surface Honeycomb worked between parallel rows of Cable.

Value: refers to the lightness or darkness of a color in relation to black and white. For example, values of red range from a very light pink to a very deep dark red, but these are all still within the same hue.

Van Dyke: the oldest of the stitches. It is worked from right to left, and two pleats are picked up at a time, an old and a new pleat. It is best to work each stitch to one-half space height.

Van Dyke Zigzag (Double Van Dyke): it is

worked at one-half-space intervals and builds to various height. It is used to form "squared" waves and pyramids.

Warm Colors: reds, oranges, yellows, and most browns. These tend to advance and appear larger.

Waves: parallel rows of any Zigzag stitch worked adjacent to each other.

Wheat Stitch: adjacent rows of Outline and Stem.

Zigzag Stitches: the stitches that are worked in the spaces between the gathering threads. (Chevron, Trellis, Surface Honeycomb, Honeycomb, Herringbone, Van Dyke, Feather)

SOURCES

For a complete list of smocking supplies write:
Little Miss Muffet
(or Rainbow Hill)
P. O. Box 10912
Knoxville, Tennessee 37919

Fashionetics Color Wheel
Fashionetics, Inc.
Box 146
Ormonk, New York 10504

METRIC CONVERSION TABLE

1 meter is about 3 feet 3 inches
10 centimeters are about 4 inches
1 centimeter is about 2/5 inch
1 millimeter is about 1/25 inch

To Convert	Multiply	By
inches to centimeters	inches	2.54
centimeters to inches	centimeters	0.39
yards to meters	yards	.9
meters to yards	meters	1.1

SEWING REFERENCE BOOKS

MacTaggart, Ann. *Complete Book of Dressmaking.* New York: Van Nostrand Reinhold Company, 1975.

Margolis, Adele P. *Design Your Own Dress Patterns.* New York: Doubleday and Co., 1971.

The New Vogue Sewing Book. Linnea Leedham, ed. New York: Butterick Publishing, 1980.

Whole Sewing Catalog. The editors of Consumer Guide.

INDEX